So,
You Want to Write
A
Fantasy
Book?

Part I

Stefan Coleman

The Adventure Begins...

So, you want to write a fantasy book, eh? Have you thought about it for a while, or has a rush of inspiration hit you and now you feel called to respond? Have you got a cool idea in mind, characters you want to take the page, an antagonist that will put Darth Vader to shame, and a setting to rival Middle Earth, or are you still figuring those out? If you're one of the ones still figuring things out, awesome, you might get the most out of this book, and I encourage you to stick around to the end. If you already have some of these in mind, well, I think this can help make them more.

All stories come down to this: Someone somewhere did something for some reason, and it was worth telling. The "someone" is your character. The "somewhere" is your setting. The "did something" is your plot. The "some reason" is your antagonist. Therefore, in this book, you'll find:

- Ways to develop your main character's personality, motivations, and backstory.

- Ways to develop the characters around your main character.
- Ways to flesh out your setting, including economy, government, religion, and technology.
- Ways to flesh out your antagonist, including their motivations and how they react to those they care for, those who serve them, and what good and evil looks like in your world.
- Prompts asking how your characters react to different situations.
- 50 plot ideas to give you inspiration, either as their own story or to mix and match to create something greater.
- Step by step tutorial to create your own fantasy maps, including a guide for coming up with location and character names.

One thing I will add is this is not a book on how to write. This is not a book on how to edit. This is not a book on how to get published. There are books like that out there, so if that's what you need, get that. This is a book about creating the story, and making you think about things you either haven't thought about or didn't think were important, because those are the things that give your world and your people character. That all being said, this is also a work book, so... buckle up.

I spend a lot of time on your main character, because, well, they're the main character. They're going to drive the plot, so having a good understanding of them will help you figure out where you want them to go. With that in mind, really think about these questions, and have fun discovering these aspects of your character's life. Take the first question, for example. I don't ask what the main character's name is, I ask where they got their name. I ask about their hobbies, their friends, their goals, and even their favorite flower. All the questions I ask help to bring out their personality and their motivations, and hopefully give you an idea of where the character wants to go in life. Some of these things are just for your benefit, and that's perfectly fine, but sometimes these little bits of info make their way

INTO THE MAIN STORY, WHICH READERS LIKE DISCOVERING.

AFTER THE MAIN CHARACTER, I WILL ASK YOU ABOUT THEIR FRIENDS. DO THEY HAVE FRIENDS? HOW MANY FRIENDS DO THEY HAVE? WE ARE DEFINED BY THE FRIENDS WE KEEP, FOR BETTER AND FOR WORSE, SO KNOWING WHO IS AROUND TO INFLUENCE THEM WILL ALSO GIVE YOU AN IDEA OF WHAT ENCOURAGEMENT THEY'LL HAVE. FRIENDS ALSO MEAN FAMILIES, WHICH NOW HELPS YOU DISCOVER THE COMMUNITY, AND DIFFERENT PERSONALITIES MEAN DIFFERENT LIKES AND INTERESTS, SO HAVE FUN WITH THOSE, TOO. ALL THE QUESTIONS FOR THE MAIN CHARACTER CAN EASILY BE USED TO BRING OUT YOUR SIDE CHARACTERS, AND OFTEN, IT'S THE SIDE CHARACTERS READERS REALLY FALL IN LOVE WITH.

THEN WE GET INTO SETTING. HONESTLY, WORLDBUILDING IS ONE OF MY FAVORITE PARTS OF WRITING FANTASY, AND I LOVE GETTING INTO HOW THE WORLD WORKS. THIS INCLUDES ECONOMY, TECHNOLOGY, MEDICINE, RELIGION, GOVERNMENT, NATURE, AND OF COURSE, MAGIC AND THE SUPERNATURAL. IT'S REALLY EASY TO SAY THOSE ELEMENTS WILL BE THE SAME EVERYWHERE YOU GO, BUT THAT'S NOT NECESSARILY THE CASE. FOR EXAMPLE, WHEN A STORY TAKES PLACE ON EARTH, WE HAVE TO DECIDE WHAT PART OF EARTH, WHAT COUNTRY, WHAT CITY, WHAT TIME OF YEAR, EVEN. THE UNITED STATES AND GREAT BRITAIN BOTH SPEAK

ENGLISH, BUT THE TWO COUNTRIES HAVE COMPLETELY DIFFERENT CULTURE. TEXAS AND ALASKA ARE BOTH STATES IN THE UNITED STATES, BUT THE CLIMATE IS COMPLETELY DIFFERENT IN BOTH. HAVE FUN DISCOVERING THE DIFFERENT PARTS OF YOUR WORLD, AND THE DIFFERENT NATIONS THAT MAKE IT UNIQUE.

THEN WE GET INTO OUR ANTAGONIST, BECAUSE WHO DOESN'T LIKE A GOOD BAD GUY. OPPOSITION IS ONE OF THE BEST TOOLS WE AS PEOPLE USE TO GROW, AND THE SAME IS TRUE FOR YOUR CHARACTERS. ANTAGONISTS COME IN ALL SHAPES AND SIZES, RANGING FROM THE GREAT AND POWERFUL SAURON FROM LORD OF THE RINGS, DOWN TO LOBELIA SACKVILLE BAGGINS. SAURON WAS THE GREAT ANTAGONIST, BRINGING HIS WAR ON ALL THE FREE PEOPLE OF MIDDLE EARTH, WITH THE DESIRE TO CONQUER AND ENSLAVE EVERYONE. LOBELIA WAS UPSET THAT SHE WOULDN'T INHERIT BILBO'S HOME WHEN HE LEFT AND WAS SNOBBY TOWARDS FRODO AS A RESULT. BOTH ANTAGONISTS WERE DEALT WITH IN THE END, BUT IN MUCH DIFFERENT WAYS AND WITH DIFFERENT OUTCOMES. IN HERE, I HELP YOU FIGURE OUT WHO THOSE ANTAGONISTS ARE, WHAT THEIR MOTIVATIONS ARE, WHAT KINDS OF PEOPLE OR THINGS THEY CARE ABOUT, AND I ALSO HELP YOU EXPLORE THE IDEA OF GOOD AND EVIL.

THEN I GIVE YOU SOME WHAT-IF SCENARIOS, AND THESE GET INTO THE CHARACTERS' MINDS IN REALLY INTERESTING WAYS. FOR EXAMPLE, IF I ASKED YOU IF YOU COULD HAVE ANY SUPERPOWER, WHAT WOULD IT BE? I'M

SURE SOMETHING POPPED INTO YOUR HEAD, AND I'M SURE IT WOULDN'T BE SURPRISING TO LEARN THAT OTHER PEOPLE HAVE OTHER IDEAS. THE LIKELIHOOD OF US ACTUALLY GETTING SUPERPOWERS IS PRETTY SLIM, BUT WE STILL LIKE TO THINK ABOUT IT. WELL, IF YOUR CHARACTER COULD HAVE ANY SUPERPOWER, WHAT WOULD IT BE? EVERY CHARACTER IS GOING TO ANSWER DIFFERENTLY. EVEN BETTER, IN YOUR BOOK, THEY MAY ACTUALLY HAVE THIS DREAM REALIZED. THESE PROMPTS ARE TO HELP PUT YOU IN YOUR CHARACTER'S MINDSET AND RESPOND TO A SITUATION THEY MIGHT ENCOUNTER. THEY MIGHT ALSO PROVE USEFUL IF YOU'VE FOUND YOURSELF AT A BIT OF A WRITER'S BLOCK AND WANT TO MOVE THE PLOT FORWARD.

SO, YOU'VE GOT YOUR CHARACTERS, YOU'VE GOT YOUR BAD GUY, YOU'VE GOT THE SETTING... WHAT ARE YOU GOING TO DO WITH THEM? MOST OF THE TIME A STORY IDEA STARTS WITH A PLOT IN MIND, BUT SOMETIMES AS YOU'RE DEVELOPING YOUR CHARACTERS, NEW PLOTS SUDDENLY BECOME COOL. DON'T JUST DROP THE OLD PLOTS, THOUGH, HANG ON TO THEM AND KEEP THEM IN MIND, BUT DON'T BE AFRAID TO EXPLORE SOMETHING THAT SOUNDS BETTER. THIS IS YOUR BOOK. AS YOU GO THROUGH THESE IDEAS, YOU MIGHT BE THINKING THEY'RE EITHER IDEAS THAT WON'T WORK FOR YOUR STORY OR THEY'RE IDEAS YOU WOULD NEVER WRITE OTHERWISE. USE THEM AS WRITING EXERCISES, THEN, TO STRETCH YOUR SKILL. THEY'RE GREAT FOR GETTING OUT OF WRITER'S BLOCK BECAUSE THEY KEEP YOU WRITING.

Lastly, because fantasy books tend to not take place on earth, it's helpful to have a map so readers are able to visualize where things are relative to each other. Every artist has their own style, but since some don't quite know where to start, this book has a little tutorial to take you step by step through my process. I cover it from a practical sense, addressing various geographical features and their necessity relative to our world, but I also cover it from an artistic sense, addressing positive and negative space, the use of shading and darkening, and some different techniques for mountains and forests. I also cover naming, including country and place names as well as character names, and the research method I go through to discover and create them.

And now we come to the most difficult part, which is the writing and putting it all together. You have the characters, now see where they'll go. You have the setting, now see what happens in it. You have the antagonist, now see how they cause problems. You have the tools, now let's see what you can build!

Main Character

Where did your main character get their name?

This is more than just how did you as the author decide on their name. In the context of the world you created, someone named this character, whether it be their parents, relatives, the orphanage they grew up in, etc. Names are often similar to their parents, like in Lord of the Rings. Names also have meanings, and kids are named how they are because of the meaning behind said name.

Does your world have a way they name characters, or is it just random? All these factors will play into how not just your main character is named, but everyone in your story.

Where did your main character grow up?

All characters grow up somewhere. Some grow up in one place, while some grow up in many. Some grow up where they're born, and sometimes they are born in one place and moved to another. This is important because where a character grew up greatly affects things like personality, connections, interests, friends, traditions, and beliefs.

This is also important, because the story has to start somewhere, and it's likely going to start where the main character is. There are exceptions to this, of course, but most likely, the place they grew up will play some part in the story you create. This also helps give you the first steps in creating the world of your story and what kinds of places and lands will be in it.

____

____

____

____

____

____

____

____

____

____

____

Who are your main character's parents?

Everyone has parents, because biologically we come from a mother and a father, who in turn came from a mother and father, etc. This is important because it addresses the character's biological origin, for example, one parent may be an elf and the other a human, resulting in a half-elf. Or one parent could be a foreign prince and the other a commoner, making the child of noble blood. Or one parent could be a dragon, and the resulting kid has powers that awaken at some point.

On that note, who actually raised this character? Was it two parents in a stable home? Was one or both of the parents absent, resulting in a hole in the child's history? Were the people who raised them not related by blood, but loved them like they were? This in turn will affect how the character sees and forms relationships, which is important if they're going to encounter any other characters down the line.

How many siblings does your main character have?

Naturally, when people have one kid, they'll often have another. Whether the kids know about each other or not, however, remains to be said.

In some cases, the character may be an only child, but in other cases they're going to have a brother or sister they grew up with. Sometimes the character will have half siblings or step siblings, or sometimes if they were abandoned and raised by someone else, there may be siblings they've never met and will discover later on in life. Sometimes the siblings aren't biological.

Regardless, whether they've met them or not, how many siblings does your character have, and did they grow up with some or all of them?

____

____

____

____

____

____

____

____

____

____

What kind of relationship does your main character have with their siblings?

Siblings can be your best friends or your worst enemies. There are many stories about brothers and sisters teaming up to accomplish amazing things, and there are stories about how siblings are pitted against each other to fight for an inheritance or the throne.

Your character might have siblings and have whatever rivalries or alliances they do, but through the course of the story decide they want something different. Or, if your character had no siblings, they might long for that kind of relationship, and use that longing to create other connections with other characters.

Whatever the relationship, think about it.

What is your main character's favorite place?

Everyone has places they like to be, whether it be at home, a park, a coffee shop, a theatre. The place could be something that comes every year but isn't permanent. The place could even be in a car, not something fixed.

However, this place is important because it could be a place your character is trying to get to, trying to protect, or constantly goes to. Also, with this question is why is this place important to your character? It could be a place they feel safe. It could be a place they feel at peace. It could be a place they feel happy. It could be where they feel free.

Thinking about what and why this place is important for your character helps you realize what's important to them.

____

____

____

____

____

____

____

____

____

____

What Job Does Your Main Character Have?

Everyone does something. They could be retail workers. They could be engineers. They could be teachers. They could be students. They could be unemployed. Whatever they do, this is going to affect many things.

A person's job or position in society will affect how people see them and how they respect them. It will help determine what a person's skills and abilities are or highlight their weaknesses. It will affect how much or how little money and possessions they have, and also affect what kind of free time they have.

Furthermore, the job they have will determine the kind of people around the character on a regular basis, whether they be workers or customers.

____

____

____

____

____

____

____

____

____

____

What hobbies does your main character have?

When you're not working or sleeping, what do you like to do? Hobbies are interesting, because not only are they things we want to do, but they're also things we want to invest time into, which develop unique skills and connections in kind.

Hobbies can include things like reading, hiking, gaming, watching movies, writing, painting, hanging out with friends, and playing sports. Figuring what kinds of hobbies your character has will help you determine what kinds of things are available in the world, and whether your character has time for leisure or not. And if they don't have time, what kinds of hobbies would they like to take up?

____

____

____

____

____

____

____

____

____

____

Who is your main character's best friend?

Some characters have many friends. Some characters have only a few friends. Only one can be their best friend. Well, who the heck are they?

People are going to be drawn towards other people for many reasons, so think about not only who this character is, but also who they are in relation to your main character. Are they similar in appearance or different? Are they the same age or different? Are they the same race or different?

Figuring out your character's best friend will also help you figure out the kinds of people around them, thus helping to shape culture and community.

____

____

____

____

____

____

____

____

____

____

____

What does your main character want to do when they're older?

As kids, we go to school and dream about our future occupations. We play sports and dream about making it into the big leagues. We look out at the world and dream about where we want to travel. We look at a person and dream of having a family.

Having this end goal gives us as people something to strive for, an end game we want to achieve. It will shape the steps we need to take, the skills we need to develop, and the wealth we need to acquire, and it's the exact same for your characters.

Some people and characters will change their dreams as they get older, and that's perfectly alright. What's most important is that they have that dream in mind to push their story forward.

____
____
____
____
____
____
____
____
____

What are your main character's goals?

Goals can be big, and goals can be small. Goals can be as simple as wanting to get a load of laundry done in the day, or as lofty as having a best seller by the time you're fifty.

You might be wondering why it matters for the character to have goals if there's already a plot in play. This is because a character with their own goals will feel more like a person to the reader and less like a means to an end. If the character has their own goals, the reader will be more invested in seeing the character achieve them, and by extension more invested in the story.

If a reader genuinely cares about a character, they will be much more inclined to stick around to the end of the story.

____

____

____

____

____

____

____

____

____

____

Is Your Main Character in a Relationship?

People love love. People love seeing characters they care about being in love because it makes the characters happy. Relationships also show that a character is capable of those kinds of feelings, and no matter how terrible of a person the character can be, you can still feel for someone in love.

Relationships often make for simple but effective side plots, whether it be a character starting a relationship, taking the relationship to the next level, taking care of a family, or letting go of someone who has become toxic. They're important for characters because they're something a reader can relate to, which by extension makes them relate to the character. If they empathize with a character, they're more invested in the story as a whole.

____

____

____

____

____

____

____

____

____

What is your main character's favorite color?

Colors are interesting because they create images. Red is often associated with passion, courage, and aggression, while blue is cooler, calmer, or more focused. White is associated with good and black associated with evil. Yellow is associated with joy, green is associated with life, brown is associated with common, and purple is associated with royalty.

However, as you read those colors, likely some other image went through your head, and possibly some people came to mind, so capitalize on that. Think about what colors your characters would like, and then think about how that would manifest in the book. Does your character decorate with a certain color? Do they dress in a certain color? Are they drawn to a certain color gem? Do they dye their hair a certain color?

____

____

____

____

____

____

____

____

____

What article of clothing does your main character like to wear?

Just like color, some characters are known by a specific article of clothing or clothing style. This might be a hat or a long coat. It might be a pair of bracers, or a gawdy belt buckle.

What's interesting about this is it might be something other people in the world are aware of. There might be rumors of a man in a wide-brimmed hat, or the lady with the orange gloves, and that invokes fear. Or, you could have a kid walk up to a grizzled old man because the kid's mother once said before she died that he could always trust someone who wore a white cloak and red boots.

Even if this isn't something anyone else in the world would know, it does help the reader be able to think about the character and create a mental picture of them, and in turn, remember them.

____

____

____

____

____

____

____

____

____

What Is Your Main Character's Favorite Flower?

Flowers give the world color and make it a better, more enjoyable place. Adding flowers to a scene, in turn, gives it color and life, and is a quick way to invoke images for the reader.

Your characters will have seen flowers of some kind, and they're going to enjoy one, whether it's because of its color, smell, shape, or memories associated with it. Or it's possible your character doesn't like any flower. In either case, think about why they like or don't like a certain flower, think about the memories the flower brings up, and use that to help shape your character's personality.

____

____

____

____

____

____

____

____

____

____

____

____

What is your main character's favorite food?

People eat. It's one of the necessity elements of life, but not all food is created equal, and some just tastes better than others.

Restaurants, taverns, and inns play important parts in many fantasy books and games, notably as gathering places, safe havens, or businesses, and one of the first things they do is order a meal. Characters will find jobs or contacts at inns and taverns, bonding over a drink, and sometimes what a character is served will reflect the relationship they have. One notable instance was how Frodo met Strider at the Prancing Pony.

When thinking about your character's favorite food, is this something they cook for others, or is cooked for them? Is it a dish that is common, or one that is served for special occasions? Or is it a dish that's only a favorite because of its association with one character? Think not only about the taste of the food, but also the memories around it.

____

____

____

____

____

____

____

How does your main character feel about magic?

Magic is almost synonymous with fantasy, so it logically follows that if your book is a fantasy, then there will be a magical element to it. This magic could be very visible, such as a character casting a fireball, moving objects with telekinesis, or causing plants to grow at a ridiculous rate. It could also be much more subtly, such as an elf's long life and uncanny accuracy, a hobbit's ability to sneak and hide in the woods effortlessly, or a dwarf's exceptional craftmanship.

However magic manifests in your world, your character will have an opinion of it, whether they're fascinated, afraid, or nonchalant. Is it commonplace, or a rarity? Does everyone possess magic, or do only a few? Does your character want to learn magic, or stay as far from it as possible?

The views your character has towards magic are likely going to be shared by others around them, so use this to also think about the role of magic in the world around them.

____

____

____

____

____

____

____

Does your main character believe in the supernatural?

In a world where there are many gods and clerics performing miraculous deeds, it would be pretty hard for a character to not believe the gods exist. However, if a character grew up around none of that, it would be easy for them to believe either there were no gods, or that the gods didn't care about them.

Has your character had a supernatural experience, like seeing a miracle happen, seeing a ghost, or hearing voices in their mind? What was their response? Have they been told about a deity and developed their faith through learning and discovery, or have they rejected everything they can't tangibly feel and sense?

____

____

____

____

____

____

____

____

____

____

____

Does Your Main Character Like to Work?

They say when you find a job you love, you never have to work a day in your life. I can say honestly that when I care about a project, it is one of the most fun things to do, and I can put in long hours, sleepless nights, and be happy. On the other hand, I've had jobs where just working a couple hours into an eight-hour shift is torture.

Some people do not like to work, however. They want things handed to them, something for nothing, and whether it's because they've only ever experienced terrible jobs, they feel work is beneath them, or for some other reason, some people are just content with existing.

If your character likes to work, they'll be the type willing to put time into a journey, willing to spend time training, willing to spend time researching, and willing to develop relationships. Those slow moments are great for readers. However, if your character does not like to work, then it's likely that there will be less character growth, which is fine for short pieces, but not so fine for longer works.

____

____

____

____

____

____

HOW DOES YOUR MAIN CHARACTER RESPOND TO AUTHORITY?

There are people who follow the law without question, and people who feel that anyone preventing them from doing whatever they want belongs in the lowest level of Hell. Most people fall in between.

However, everyone has their own reasons, and often this question is going to be situational. For example, a teacher who only believes themselves to be correct even when proven wrong may be hated and rebelled against, while a teacher who makes you feel respected is one you'll fight for. A general who fights on the front lines with their troops will be loved, while one who orders from a safe distance will be disliked. A leader who believes in an equal distribution of wealth will be loved by those who don't contribute and have nothing, and hated by those who worked for and earned what they got.

Think about the kind of people your character respects, the kinds of rules they want to follow, and why.

____

____

____

____

____

____

Who is a person your main character respects?

It's not uncommon that there is going to be someone that a person looks up to, whether it's someone they want to be, someone who did something for them, or someone they can get something from.

Mentors are very powerful characters narratively because they offer support, knowledge, skill, inspiration, guidance, but sometimes their most important role is to show where the main character is lacking and how they can grow.

Character growth is important, especially in longer pieces, and having a person the character can learn from in a positive way is a great way to do that.

One thing to note, though this character is often older, having a younger person the character admires can be very powerful, too, so don't necessarily feel this has to be a wizened old man.

____

____

____

____

____

____

____

____

____

____

Does Your Main Character Like to Read?

If you're here, you obviously know the value books have, and you probably also like to read. Some people hate to read though, which is very unfortunate for them.

In this day and age, most people have access to books, but a few hundred years ago that wasn't the case. Before the printing press, books were recorded manually. Yeah, think about that. Well, in a fantasy setting, it's possible that there aren't printing presses, so any books available are literally hand copied. In that setting books will be few and far between.

Think about your character's experience with books and literature. Do they like books, or are books a bore? Can they even read and write at all? Are there certain things your character likes to read but not others, or is all knowledge regarded as amazing?

____

____

____

____

____

____

____

____

____

____

How important is money to your main character?

Love it or hate it, economics is vital to the success of a nation, city, town, or village. However, not everyone uses money, and not everyone needs money.

For some, money is the goal, and acquiring the most money means acquiring the most stuff, and by extension, winning at life. For others, money is a means to an end, a way to fund travel, a way to fund school or training, or a way to afford a break. Still others despise money and prefer to give goods or services in exchange for necessities and choose to craft or gather resources on their own.

Some characters are going to come from wealthy backgrounds where money is readily available, and some will come from a modest upbringing where all coin is fought hard for. There will also be poor characters completely content, and rich characters who never have enough. Where does your character sit?

____

____

____

____

____

____

____

____

What Does Your Main Character Dream About?

During the day, our dreams are an escape, and we dream about everything from future plans, travels, things we want to make, people we want to see, relationships we want to have, what kind of superpower we would have , etc. However, at night, they say our dreams are reflections of what we really want, what we really care about, whether we know it or not.

Look at this question both ways. During the day, is their head always in the clouds, or are they down to earth? Do they have plans and goals for the future, or do they just want to take each day at a time? Do they have an ending they're working towards, or do they not care?

During the night, is there a dream that plagues them often, or are their sleeps dreamless? Does a foreign entity speak to them in their dreams, or do they have the ability to go into other people's dreams?

____

____

____

____

____

____

____

____

What does your main character regret?

Regret can be terrible, but it can also be a powerful motivator. Some people stay in their regret and can't move forward from it, while some remember the regret and use it to not have regrets in the future.

Regret could come in the form of not telling someone they love them. It could be regret at gambling away their house. It could be regret for quitting a sport too early. It could be regret at not applying for a certain job.

Is there something your character wishes they had done or not done? What was it? Is there a way to fix that problem, or has that opportunity passed? One reason readers love watching characters right wrongs is because it encourages them to fix things they may have done, and sometimes seeing a character they admire facing their fears gives them the courage to face theirs.

____

____

____

____

____

____

____

____

____

How does your main character feel about nobility and royalty?

Some places have people of royal and noble blood, but not everywhere. In some places royals are the people in command, in other places, they're figureheads, and in other places they rule with a government of commoners. Still other places, they're the enemy of the people, and there are many stories about the citizens overthrowing a lord or king.

In places where nobles have a prominent presence, your character may have actually interacted with them in some way. Has the experience been positive or negative? Is your character a noble themselves and their life has been surrounded by them? Does your character believe being noble gives them a right to rule, or a responsibility?

____

____

____

____

____

____

____

____

____

____

What is your main character afraid of?

I had an English teacher say that we learn a lot about society by studying what society is afraid of. In a fantasy world, there are a lot of supernatural things to be afraid of, but take away the magic and you really get to the core of their fear.

Are they afraid of a tyrannical lord? Are they afraid of a beast that only comes out at night? Are they afraid of some god or demon? Are they afraid of the dark? Are they afraid of the water? Are they afraid of the future?

Now think why they are afraid of what they're afraid of. Some things provide a rational reason to be afraid. The beast that comes out at night is a very real threat, but said beast could cultivate a fear of the dark in general, even if said beast is defeated. A fear of enclosed spaces could stem from a time they were locked in a small room as a child. A fear of a demon could be because of a story told when they were younger.

Is Your Main Character Well Liked?

Some people are more liked than others. You probably like some people more than others. Think about why they're liked.

Some people are liked because they're wealthy. Some people are liked because of their connections, rank, or positions. Some people are liked for their courage and skill. Some people are liked for their kindness. And some people are liked for some unperceived reason, but they just seem to be. Think about this for your character.

Being well liked does not necessarily mean they have a lot of close friends. Some people keep a small circle while some keep a large circle. Think about what kind of person you want your character to be, and then think about why they're received the way they are.

Does Your Main Character Make Friends Easily?

Some people have crowds around them, and everyone is welcome in. Some people don't want a lot of people, preferring only a few confidants. Some people want more friends but just don't know how to go about it.

In a lot of stories, we like to see our main character able to make friends easily, because friends mean allies and support and aid and resources, and we want our characters to have everything they want. That's not always the case, though, and sometimes seeing the struggle to make one or a certain friend is a draw to readers.

When thinking about whether or not they can make friends easily, think also if they want a lot of friends or not.

Does Your Main Character Have Any Enemies?

There are many stories where a dark lord killed the parents of the main character and now their goal is to defeat that enemy. There are many stories where a good character wants to defeat all evil, making the most evil being their greatest enemy. Sometimes a character is just on the other side of a war as the main character, making them an enemy for no other reason than they belong to different sides.

Whatever the reason, an enemy is someone your character actively tries to defeat, so if there is such a character, think about why they are an enemy. Why does your character want to defeat them? Do they need to defeat them? What would happen if they weren't defeated?

____

____

____

____

____

____

____

____

____

____

What is your main character skilled at?

This should probably speak for itself, but what is your character good at? Are they skilled at hunting? Are they skilled with a sword? Are they skilled at stealing stuff? Skills are important for characters to have, sure, however, there are other ways to look at this.

For example, is your character skilled at calming down after being angered? Are they skilled at finding information through research? Are they skilled at reading body language? Are they skilled at thinking in ways other people don't? Are they skilled at cleaning?

Some skills are not going to seem obvious for a story, but having them gives the character depth, and they sometimes provide unique solutions to seemingly unsolvable problems.

____

____

____

____

____

____

____

____

____

What Are Your Main Character's Flaws?

If the answer to this question is "none, my characters aren't flawed," it would be very wise to revisit them. Flaws, or hinderances, are things that hold the character back in some way, and readers like to watch the characters overcome them. They're necessary for a good character, because readers relate to flawed characters, which in turn makes them care about them, and therefore care about your book. Flaws aren't necessarily evil, either. For example, being short doesn't make a character bad, but it does prevent them from reaching the top shelf.

One of my creative writing classmates shared how, "with heroes, give them one vice for every two virtues, and for villains, give them one virtue for every two vices. You can make your strong, courageous hero insecure, and you can take your evil, bloodthirsty vampire and give him a puppy." This is a good rule of thumb, because people are not going to be perfect, and it's hard to relate to a perfect character. The bit about the villains is good, though, because if there aren't any virtues, they're not going to be believable.

____

____

____

____

____

____

How does your main character treat someone weaker than them?

They say you can tell a lot about a person by how they treat those who are beneath them. Some characters, if they are stronger than another, will constantly try to put that character down and try to keep them below them. Others will see a weaker character but treat them as equals. Still others will choose to mentor and train said character.

Think about who your character is. If they're insecure, they may try to put down everyone in an attempt to not be the lowest. If they're confident in who they are, they'll be glad to bring someone up.

___

___

___

___

___

___

___

___

___

___

___

How does your main character treat someone less intelligent than them?

Not everyone is as smart as everyone else. Being purely technical, just because of how math works, half of the people of the world are going to be above average intelligence and half are below average intelligence. Some people seem to take great offense at people of lesser intelligence being in the room with them or enjoy lording their intelligence over them. Others just see people as people, focusing on the strengths they have instead.

Think about your character. Are they above average intelligence, average, or below average? What about in their friend group? Are they patient and accepting or do they get irritated or disdainful, and do they show it? Do they push people down, or pull people up?

____

____

____

____

____

____

____

____

____

How does your main character treat someone stronger than them?

Some people look at people stronger than them and treat them like heroes. They see them as people who can protect them and feel safe around them. Others look at strong people and see them as what they can aspire to be. They spend their lives trying to be that person. Still others see strong people and hate them for being that way. There is what is called small man syndrome, or people with a Napoleon Complex, who try to over compensate with overly aggressive behavior.

Think about your character, though. Are they naturally small, or are they already strong? Are there many people stronger than them, or are there very few? Do they try to get stronger, or bring others down?

____

____

____

____

____

____

____

____

How does your main character treat someone smarter than them?

Only one person can be the smartest person in the world, and odds are good your character is not them. Some people see more intelligent people as their heroes and would love the opportunity to sit with them and learn all that they can. Others, especially in a school setting, feel inferior, and take out their frustration through bullying the smarter individual.

This is not necessarily how they treat a specific person. For example, in The Big Bang Theory, Sheldon is clearly more intelligent than most people, but he's a complete jerk, and generally treats people considerably less intelligent with disdain. Leonard, on the other hand, values the person, and tries to keep conversation on a level the other person can engage on (though occasionally he does nerd out).

Think about your character. Do they desire to grow intellectually, or are they content where they are? Do they see people of more intelligence as an asset or a threat?

____

____

____

____

____

____

____

____

How does your main character treat someone older than them?

In the past, there was a general understanding that an older person is treated with respect. Some have taken advantage, or tried to take advantage, of that. Recently, though, there has been a shift in behavior, especially in the western world, with treating people proportional to how they are treated.

With this question, you're also thinking about the society this character is around, not just the character themself. How does your society view and treat elderly people? Are they someone to be respected, or ignored? Are they a strength to society, or a burden? Does your character act and believe in accordance with society, or are they a rebel?

____

____

____

____

____

____

____

____

____

How does your main character treat someone younger than them?

Some people see youth as the future of society, and they must therefore be nourished and trained so society will flourish. Others see youth as lesser beings who should be at the beck and call of anyone older. Some people find the energy of youth invigorating and love to be around them. Others find youth annoying, believing kids should be seen and not heard.

Whatever the view, your character will have a view, so how do they feel about someone younger than them? Do they treat them as equals or lesser citizens? Do they see them as someone deserving of their time, or not? Do they give credit where credit's due, or undermine their contributions? Are they threatened when someone younger does something better, or are they impressed?

____

____

____

____

____

____

____

____

____

Does your main character have a defining life event?

If someone were to ask what Batman's most important life event is, many people would say it was the death of his parents and watching it happen as a child. Iron Man's defining moment is when he was captured and built his first suit in captivity. Spider-man's was when his Uncle Ben died, far more than getting bit by that spider. These moments were crucial to these characters because they completely changed the character's worldview and defined how the character behaved in the future.

Some characters will have had a defining moment, but not all. Some characters have their moment later in the story, and that's really cool, too. Some characters don't have a defining moment that seems important to others, but is just important to them.

Whatever the case, think about why your character is the way they are, why they behave or think in a certain way, and think about if there was one moment in particular that caused the shift.

____

____

____

____

____

____

____

What is your main character's favorite drink?

When you go to a coffee shop, what kind of drink do you order? When you go to a restaurant, what do you get? When they don't have your choice, does it matter, or are you upset?

This is more of a flavor question for the world, but it does have some deeper implications. It's possible a character's drink order will never come up in the story, but it does provide a unique way to show the character's personality. For example, if a character's favorite drink is tea, will they insist every host serve them tea and look down on those who don't? If a character's favorite drink is Coke, how do they feel if a place only has Pepsi? If the drink doesn't taste as they expect, how do they react? Do they have such a refined pallet that they can taste if something is off with a drink they like?

____

____

____

____

____

____

____

____

____

____

SUPPORTING CHARACTERS

How did your main character and their best friend meet?

Can you remember how you and your best friend met? Are there any meetings you can remember to this day? I can know where I met many of my friends because of school or sports, but I can only remember a couple of specific instances, and those are of two friends I met back in elementary school and junior high.

With your character's best friend, not only are you creating the character, but you're also creating the relationship. You're creating the bonds that bind them together, forging the friendship, so definitely spend some time thinking about this. If two characters fight, the strength of that bond will affect how much the reader cares. If one character dies, the reader will care if they like the character, but care even more if a character they like cares.

However strong the bond is, it started somehow.

Why are your main character and their best friend actually friends?

It's one thing to meet a person. It's another thing to want to keep them around. You have probably met hundreds or thousands of people, but only a few you're actually friends with. Well, your characters are the same way.

Some people are friends because circumstances put them together and keep them in proximity with each other. Others are friends because of one defining moment. This might be the moment they met, but it might be a moment that happened long after. In a lot of stories, two characters are enemies for years, but then one moment changes things. So, what made your characters become friends? If you want to take it further, what made your characters as strong as they are?

____

____

____

____

____

____

____

____

____

How long have your main character and their best friend known each other?

As said before, some people know each other for years before becoming friends, while others meet each other and are instantly friends. You've already thought about the age of your character, where and how they grew up. Well, when did their best friend come into the picture? Have they known each other their entire lives, or have they only met recently? Bear in mind, the length of time doesn't necessarily impact the strength of their bond, but it's going to affect various events the characters experienced over their years. Therefore, as you're figuring out your character's backstory, think also how their friend or friends affected that.

___

___

___

___

___

___

___

___

___

___

What are your main character's best friend's major strengths?

You've thought about what makes your character awesome, so now think about what makes their friend awesome. Think about what your character admires about their friend, think about how their friend complements them, and think about if there are ways their friend outshines them.

In the best stories, one character can't solve every problem, and so they need to find someone who can. Sometimes a character's strength isn't enough immediately, so they need to find someone to develop it. Sometimes a character may have a specific strength only applicable for one situation, but when that situation comes, the character saves the day. The important things to remember are that every strength of every character is a tool for the author to work with to solve some problem, and one character doesn't have to do everything.

____

____

____

____

____

____

____

____

What are your main character's best friend's major weaknesses?

Just like your main character has flaws, how are their friends flawed? In some cases, a person is drawn to another because the person can do something they cannot. In other cases, a person is drawn to another because the person makes them not be ashamed of their flaws.

Some flaws can be physical, like being excessively short, which requires another character to reach that top shelf. Other flaws are mental, like having a learning disability, which requires the main character to tutor them. Other flaws, like depression, are countered by having a character around that makes you not feel as depressed.

Again, having flaws does not necessarily make the character bad. Granted, if a character enjoyed kicking puppies, that's an exception, but in general, flaws refer to things that hold the character back in some way and can be used to show another character's strength.

Some stories involve an epic fight between two characters, and in some stories, that fight is between two characters that are friends, used to be friends, or are about to be. Fights can be physically two characters using fists or weapons or armies, or it can be a disagreement in words or indirect actions. Sometimes a fight resolves an issue, but sometimes it can leave lingering resentment that never gets resolved.

Characters are always going to disagree about something, so this isn't addressing that. This is addressing an actual fight, so it's quite possible that your characters haven't actually fought. That's perfectly fine. However, did they dule in another way? Did they have an organized fist fight? Did they have a cordial, but no less passionate, debate? Were they at odds about a girl?

____

____

____

____

____

____

____

____

What other friends does your main character hang out with?

This should be self-explanatory, but what other characters are your character friends with? Why are they friends with them? How good of a friend are they to them? What role does each friend fulfill in the friends group? Spend some time thinking about them, because you may fall in love with them and spawn stories from them.

Are your main character and their friends part of the same social class?

Rich people are often friends with other rich people because they can go places poor people cannot. Poor people are often friends with poor people because the kinds of things they can do are more limited. Royalty is often friends (or rivals) with other royalty because they're around other royal people, and sometimes are actively prevented from associating with commoners.

Intentional or not, our friends are often going to be the people around us, engaging in the same activities we enjoy, and sometimes those are activities others cannot participate in.

Sometimes, though, a character breaks the mold, and a prince may sneak off to hang out with a street urchin, or a lord's son forms an alliance with a rich snob and a blacksmith's brother when they join the army.

Whatever their positions, think about how your characters stand, and how their class matters.

____

____

____

____

____

____

____

HOW OPEN ARE YOUR MAIN CHARACTER AND THEIR
FRIENDS TO INCLUDING NEW PEOPLE INTO THEIR SOCIAL
CIRCLE?

SOME PEOPLE ARE SOCIAL BUTTERFLIES, AND THE ENTIRE
WORLD IS THEIR SOCIAL CIRCLE. SOME PEOPLE ARE MUCH MORE
CLOSED OFF, AND ONLY LET A COUPLE PEOPLE IN. SOME PEOPLE
FORM SOCIAL CIRCLES OF A LIMITED NUMBER OF INDIVIDUALS, BUT
OFTEN, EVERYONE HAS THEIR OWN SOCIAL CIRCLE THEY'RE A PART
OF.

YOUR MAIN CHARACTER LIKELY HAS A GROUP OF PEOPLE
THEY LIKE TO HANG AROUND WITH, ESPECIALLY IF THEY GREW UP
IN A SMALL COMMUNITY. WHAT HAPPENS WHEN ANOTHER PERSON
IS INTRODUCED? ARE THEY BROUGHT INTO THE FOLD EASILY, OR
DOES IT TAKE SOME TIME, OR EVEN AN INITIATION PROCESS? DO
THEY LET ANYONE IN AT ALL, OR DO THEY KEEP THEM IN AN OUTER
CIRCLE?

Do the friends have dreams outside of the friends group?

Some friends follow each other through school, college, even getting jobs in the same place. For some, the group is family, and you don't do anything if it doesn't include family. However, we know that often in life, friends are going to have different passions, different life goals, and though they will always be friends, their path goes a different direction.

Think about the characters' end goals. Are they going to align with other characters or be completely different? Are they going to be different but still stay in the same town, or do their plans involve them leaving completely? Think about what the characters would do, not necessarily what you want them to do.

____

____

____

____

____

____

____

____

____

____

Setting

What is the name of the country your story takes place in?

Gondor. Rohan. Narnia. The Shire. Some stories exist in a set country, a set land, and adventure in that land, while some stories travel to other nations. Sometimes, they even go to other worlds.

Even if your story starts in a single town, and they only travel to places in that town, that town is going to exist in a country or an area that was a country once. If it's part of a country, there will likely be connections with the main country, but if it's part of a country that used to exist, then some of the traditions, mannerisms, weaponry, architecture, appearances, etc. may have carried over.

Think about where your story is in the world, and how that affects the story as a whole.

What is the role of magic in your world?

In some settings, magic is the lifeblood of the world. In other settings magic is just one other force that exists. Still, in other worlds, magic is something to be reviled and rejected.

Magic has many possible purposes, including granting long life, granting superhuman abilities, healing, allowing for flight or teleportation, and manipulating the world around them.

When creating your world, decide what magic looks like, whether it's recognized as magic or not. Think, also, about how it's perceived by other people, the kinds of people who practice it, and how they're perceived and regarded.

____

____

____

____

____

____

____

____

____

____

____

What are the Major Religions in Your World?

In a world of magic and gods, there will be people believing in, or not believing in, whatever they want. When there are gods healing people, there will be followers. When there are gods providing power, there will be followers. When there are people possessing amazing abilities, there will be followers.

Whether the religion is true or not, there will be people believing in it because they want to. So, in your world, what do people believe? Is there a pantheon of deities that everyone worships, or are their different religions around each deity? Do people worship nature itself, or some aspect of nature? Do people worship idols? A concept? Themselves? Anything at all?

____

____

____

____

____

____

____

____

____

____

Are gods real in your world?

A religion may worship a god or gods, but that doesn't mean the gods are real or who they say they are. There are countless instances where individuals or evil entities have declared themselves gods to gain followers, or to wage war against the actual gods, so think about your own world. Are there gods in your world that created the world? Are there false gods trying to gain followers? Is there one God?

____

____

____

____

____

____

____

____

____

____

____

____

____

What are the largest cities in your story's main country?

Thinking about our world, most people will have heard of New York City in the United States. Most of the world will know of London, England, as well as Paris, France, and Tokyo, Japan. However, not a lot of people will have heard of Anchorage, Alaska, because compared to the rest, it's pretty small.

In your world, think about the major cities, because these will be the cities that other countries will know of. Sometimes there are going to be many cities that are huge, but sometimes there's going to be only one, or maybe there are none that would be considered a big city.

Once you have the biggest city figured out, think about how big that city is, and then think about a few other smaller cities that will be known in that country. This is an easy way to start forming your world.

____

____

____

____

____

____

____

____

____

____

How big of a city does your main character come from?

There's almost a romanticism behind having your main character come from a small village and humble origins only to rise to become a powerful figure in the world. And to be fair, people like reading it. However, not every main character has to start in a small town.

When thinking about where your character grew up, think about how big of a community that actually is as well as how prominent they are in that community. From a comic standpoint, Superman came from Smallville, while Batman came from Gotham City. Smallville is very small, simple, and humble, while Gotham City is about the size of modern New York City. Both are popular heroes (arguable who is the most popular), but both come from drastically different origins.

____

____

____

____

____

____

____

____

____

____

What is your main country known for?

Some countries are known for something that happened in their history. Some are known for their geography. Some are known for their beliefs. Some are known for a single person.

When thinking about your story's main country, is there anything in particular that would make another country think about them? Was there a great war they were known for? A powerful leader? Are they doing something at the present to make themselves known?

____

____

____

____

____

____

____

____

____

____

____

____

____

What kind of money does your main country use?

Money is useful in the exchanging of goods and services because it's a currency people can use as a unifier. For example, if a person wanted to buy a goat in exchange for grain, the goat seller might not want to trade because they don't need the grain. The goat seller might need someone to repair their roof instead, but the repairman may not consider their service worth the same amount of grain, or even worth grain at all. With money, however, the grain has a value, the goat has a value, and the service has a value, all in the same medium.

Historically, a lot of places used gold, silver, and copper, and paper money came into play as promissory notes, or notes that had a value of gold tied to them. Said notes could then be brought to a bank and exchanged for the amount listed. How does your story's currency and economy work? Do they use coins or notes, or are they on a barter system, or something else entirely?

____

____

____

____

____

____

____

____

Who rules your main country?

Government is actually quite fascinating. How is it determined who has the right to rule? Some believe in the idea that "might is right," or the strongest person holds all the power. In a religious society, the person divinely blessed or decreed by a deity is the rightful ruler. In a democracy, what the people want, they get. In an anarchy, no one rules anyone.

The strength of a nation is directly tied to the strength of its leadership. If the country is united under a single leader, that leader can direct the country in a very focused way. If the government is divided, then it's harder to steer the country in any direction, and if everyone is doing their own thing, then it's not really a nation.

Think about what kind of government your country has, whether it be monarchy (rule of one), oligarchy (rule of a few), democracy (rule by majority of people), republic (rule by representatives of people), or something else.

____

____

____

____

____

____

____

WHO ARE YOUR MAIN COUNTRY'S ALLIES?

They say no man is an island. Well, while it's true that a country may be an island, they still exist in the world, and thus are a part of the world. It's very unlikely that your nation is completely isolated from every other nation, which means they're either allied to, neutral with, or enemies towards the other nations around them.

Alliances can come in various forms. Often it has to do with war and protection, with one country pledging to come to the other's defense if either is attacked or goes to war. Other alliances are focused on trade meant to benefit each other's economies.

Therefore, what kinds of alliances exist with your main country, and why are or were said alliances established?

____

____

____

____

____

____

____

____

____

____

Is your main country more coastal or inland?

A lot of this question will be determined by the size of your country, so if this question seems odd, bear with me. Some countries are right in the middle of a continent, with no ocean access whatsoever, so obviously they're more inland. Other countries are made up of islands, so obviously they're more coastal.

A better way to think about this is how important is the ocean to your country. For some nations, the ocean is a primary means of travel, food production, economic development, and military dominance. Some nations have powerful navies and others have weak ones. Some nations have multiple trade routes, others have few.

Nations that place a high importance on the coast will have their larger cities on the coast, while nations that don't will have their larger cities more inland.

Does your story take place on the coast or more inland?

Focusing back on the story itself, does your story have more of the page time on the ocean or coast, or more inland? Thinking about Lord of the Rings, they spend very little time on the coast, pretty much cutting right through the middle of Middle Earth. On the other hand, Twenty Thousand Leagues Under the Seas is primarily on or under the water.

This is going to affect a lot of things, such as the setting, people, people groups, skills, food, etc. This is also going to affect your readership. In one of my creative writing classes, one girl rated my story less because she didn't like stories with an oceanic lean. That is perfectly fine, just be prepared that whichever direction you take, people will have opinions, and not all opinions are going to be helpful.

____

____

____

____

____

____

____

____

What are the major imports and exports of your main country?

Countries need wealth to come in to grow, but sometimes they need other resources because said resources are either not available, or not available in the quantities they want.

Tolkien made a point of saying when the dwarf kingdoms were in their prime, they traded their crafts and ores for food, so they didn't need to produce it themselves. We know the dwarves were fully capable of producing their own food, but if they can get it cheaper elsewhere, then why not?

Sometimes a nation has stores of a unique metal or gem. Sometimes a coastal nation will trade marine produce for grain. Sometimes a nation will loan out their military in exchange for coin and goods.

Whatever it is, think about what your nation has an excess of and a deficiency in, and use it to shape their culture.

____

____

____

____

____

____

____

How important is your main character's city to the rest of the country?

Sometimes a person is from a place that everyone knows about, everyone travels to, and they are treated uniquely because of it. Sometimes a person is from somewhere hardly anyone else has heard of, and now they become a mystery.

Although you as the writer know this place, think about the importance it has to everyone else, not just in the context of your story. Forget the plot and get inside the head of a random character.

Is this city one well known to the country's leaders? Why is it or not? If this city was attacked or had internal problems, how long before others knew and did something about it? The "chosen one" may come from this small village, so it'll be known after they do their thing, but what about before that?

____

____

____

____

____

____

____

____

____

____

What is your main country's climate like?

Some places are tropical. Some places are dry and sandy. Some places are cold and snowy. Some places are a mix. The climate of the place is going to affect what seasons look like, what kinds of plant life grows, what kinds of animals there are, what people look like, what people wear, and what their homes are like.

Think about climate when thinking about your story. A character walking around shirtless in one-hundred-degree weather might be commonplace, but put them in a winter climate, and suddenly they're in dire straits.

____

____

____

____

____

____

____

____

____

____

____

WHEN WAS YOUR COUNTRY'S LAST MAJOR EVENT?

THINK ABOUT THE LAST MAJOR EVENT IN YOUR COUNTRY. NOT YOUR BOOK'S COUNTRY, I MEAN YOUR ACTUAL COUNTRY. WHEN WAS IT? HOW LONG AGO DID IT HAPPEN? HOW MANY PEOPLE REMEMBER IT?

SOME PEOPLE ARE DEFINED BY VARIOUS EVENTS, BECAUSE THEY ACTUALLY EXPERIENCED THEM, WHILE FOR OTHERS, IT'S JUST SOMETHING IN A TEXT BOOK. WHEN THE TWO TOWERS WERE ATTACKED, I WAS STILL IN SCHOOL. I'M A TEACHER NOW, AND IN MY CLASSES, THERE ARE NO STUDENTS ANYMORE THAT WERE BORN BEFORE 9/11 HAPPENED. A LOT CHANGED THAT DAY. I CAN STILL REMEMBER WHAT LIFE WAS LIKE, BUT NONE OF MY STUDENTS CAN BECAUSE THEY WEREN'T HERE.

THINK ABOUT HOW LONG AGO THIS EVENT HAPPENED BECAUSE IT'S GOING TO DETERMINE HOW PEOPLE BEHAVE, THINK, AND EXIST. IT'S GOING TO CREATE A DIVIDE BETWEEN PEOPLE WHO REMEMBER AND THOSE WHO DON'T, SO IF YOU WANT THE PEOPLE TO BE MORE OF THE SAME MINDSET, HAVE THE EVENT TAKE PLACE LONG IN THE PAST. IF YOU WANT CHARACTERS TO BE ABLE TO RECOLLECT THE EVENT, HOWEVER, CONSIDER HAVING IT CLOSER TO THE START OF THE STORY.

AFTER THAT, THINK ABOUT WHAT OTHER AGE GAPS THERE MIGHT BE AMONG THE PEOPLE, AND THEN CONSIDER IF THERE MIGHT BE A PROMINENT EVENT THAT WOULD HAVE CAUSED IT.

____

____

____

____

____

WHAT WAS YOUR COUNTRY'S LAST MAJOR EVENT?

ALRIGHT, SO WE KNOW WHEN YOUR EVENT HAPPENED. WELL, WHAT WAS IT? WHAT MADE IT MAJOR? HOW IMPORTANT WAS IT TO THE COUNTRY? HOW IMPORTANT WAS IT TO THE WORLD?

SOMETIMES A MAJOR EVENT IS A NATURAL DISASTER, LIKE THE ERUPTION OF A VOLCANO, A TSUNAMI, OR A DROUGHT. SOMETIMES IT'S POLITICAL, LIKE THE ELECTION/RISE/DEATH OF A LEADER, OR A WAR. SOMETIMES IT'S THE VICTORY OR LOSS OF A SPORTS TEAM. WHATEVER THE EVENT, THINK ALSO ABOUT WHAT THE EFFECTS OF SAID EVENT ARE.

THEN, LIKE BEFORE, THINK ABOUT OTHER IMPORTANT PAST EVENTS, AND THINK ABOUT HOW THEY AFFECT THE PEOPLE WHO LIVE PAST THEM.

How old is your country?

Sometimes it feels like a country has always been here, but that's the case. A country has to first be founded, cities built, borders established, leaders put in place, and then recognized by others. Countries that have been around for a long time will likely be more set in their ways, their borders firm, while younger countries are constantly changing, their borders fluctuating as wars and exploration shape their space.

If your country has been around for a while, think about the effect that will have on the people and on other nations around them. If your nation is brand new, think about if your character will be one to help shape it.

____

____

____

____

____

____

____

____

____

____

____

How are leaders determined in your country?

As we mentioned with the type of governments, how are the leaders actually determined? Is there an election, and if so, who does the electing and who can be elected? Is it a position they're born into, and if that's the case, what happens if there's no heir? Is it a position that is physically fought over, and if that's the case, how often can someone challenge the leadership?

Even though it might be something distant from your story as a whole, think about the world outside because it's going to impact things more than you realize. Leaders impact what alliances are good, which wars to fight, which programs to fund, and different leaders will have different ideas of what's important. One leader may agree completely with your hero. Another may agree with the villain.

____

____

____

____

____

____

____

____

____

WHAT KINDS OF ANIMALS ARE IN YOUR COUNTRY?

NOT EVERY ANIMAL IS IN EVERY COUNTRY, AND NOT EVERY ANIMAL IS IN EVERY PART OF THE COUNTRY. YOU'VE ALREADY THOUGHT ABOUT THE CLIMATE OF YOUR COUNTRY, SO NOW THINK ABOUT WHAT KINDS OF ANIMALS ARE IN THOSE AREAS. HOWEVER, BECAUSE THIS IS FANTASY... YOU CAN CREATE YOUR OWN!

YES, WHAT IS BEAUTIFUL ABOUT CREATING YOUR OWN WORLD IS THAT YOU CAN CREATE NEW CREATURES THAT AREN'T NECESSARILY MAGICAL. SOMETIMES THIS WILL MEAN MODIFYING EXISTING CREATURES, LIKE THEIR HAIR AND SKIN COLOR OR PHYSICAL SIZE. SOMETIMES IT WILL MEAN CHANGING THE CLIMATE THEY NORMALLY LIVE IN. SOMETIMES IT WILL MEAN ADDING TRAITS THAT AREN'T NORMALLY THERE, LIKE HORNS ON A BLACK BEAR, WINGS ON A SPIDER, OR GILLS ON A MOUSE. SOMETIMES IT WILL MEAN CHANGING AN HERBIVORE INTO A CARNIVORE, OR AN ISOLATED CREATURE INTO A PACK OR SWARM TYPE CREATURE.

WHATEVER YOU DECIDE, PEOPLE WILL USE THESE ANIMALS FOR FOOD, SKINS, PETS, AND WORK, SO THINK ABOUT WHAT WILL WORK FOR YOUR STORY.

____

____

____

____

____

____

____

What kinds of plants are in your country?

Just like animals, plants are going to be different wherever you go, so think about what that looks like. Are there trees, or do none of the plants grow more than a few feet tall? Are they leafy or covered in needles? Are they poisonous or edible? Are they decorative or practical?

A very important use of plants is as foodstuff, but a really cool use is as medicine. Sometimes a situation requires a medical solution, and many fantasy worlds are not going to have modern pharmaceuticals, so the likelihood of getting aspirin for a headache is pretty low. However, if there's a specific herb or plant people use, it'll help build the world and establish it as something a bit more fantastic.

____

____

____

____

____

____

____

____

____

You've probably realized I like flowers. What can I say, flowers bring color to a scene. When the reader is envisioning a scene, they want something to make it stand out, and flowers are a really good way to go. When all the landscape is just green trees and green grass, having a pop of color makes the scene feel a little more vibrant, especially if you show how the colors are changing as the scene moves. Even in a city setting, people grow flowers because they like how they brighten things, provide pleasant scents, and help bees. People even name others after flowers.

One thing Tolkien did in Lord of the Rings is he established a general rule of thumb where hobbit lasses are named after flowers, so I did a reverse thing where I created flowers, named them after my friends, and then included them at various places in my book. I generally don't like inserting people in as specific characters, but I like making them a part of my world, so if you're looking for a way to make your world a bit more distinct, consider doing the same.

____

____

____

____

____

____

Does gunpowder exist in your world?

A lot of people don't like the idea of gunpowder in a fantasy setting because they feel it is too modern and breaks the image of what a fantasy world is. This is completely true, and completely not.

The thing about gunpowder is that it provides a lot of possibilities, but that doesn't mean you have to have all those possibilities developed, and it doesn't mean other things can't be there. I think one misconception we have is that if there is gunpowder, then it means everyone has access to gunpowder. This might be the case, but what if gunpowder was developed by one mad scientist for the king, and it is extremely expensive to produce? Now, only the very rich will have access, and it'll be likely that a commoner will never see a gun in their lifetime.

In a world with magic, magic users may not feel them worth using, and may have even developed certain spells to counter them.

As a writer, gunpowder is just another tool you can use to develop your world. Whether you use it or not is completely up to you and whether your story would benefit from having it.

____

____

____

____

____

____

How do people travel over mountains, if they even do at all?

In our day and age, we can travel virtually anywhere on the face of the earth and can theoretically completely circumnavigate it in two days. It kind of makes Phileas Fogg a bit slow, but it does beg the question of why the heck it took him so long. Unfortunately, Fogg did not have the technology available to us today, so a lot of transportation feats we find common would be extremely difficult, or even impossible.

Mountains form a natural barrier that would prevent moving a lot of people through quickly if they were just on foot, not to mention the gear and equipment they would need. If a mountain is too steep, only a few could even climb it, so what did people often do? Often, they would just go around.

How do people travel over mountains in your world? Do they have all terrain vehicles, or even aircraft, or are they limited to hiking and pack animals? Or do they just magic themselves around? If you remember us talking about creating animals for your world, this would be a great thing to create one for.

____

____

____

____

____

____

Do books exist in your world?

We've talked a bit about whether or not your character likes to read, or even has access to books. Well, just because your character doesn't have access to them doesn't mean they don't exist.

If books exist, though, there are also a number of questions to consider. First, does the technology exist for mass production, or are all books written and copied by hand? How long does it take to make a book? How much does it cost to make a book? What kinds of people make books? Who actually owns books? Are there public libraries, private libraries, or just personal libraries?

Think also about what kinds of information people have, what people know, what the literacy rates are, and how people know what they know.

____

____

____

____

____

____

____

____

____

WHO HAS ACCESS TO WRITING IN YOUR WORLD?

SOME SOCIETIES BELIEVE THAT ALL INFORMATION SHOULD BE SHARED AND AVAILABLE TO ALL. PEOPLE KNOW HOW TO READ, AND THOUGH SOME INFORMATION IS TOO ADVANCED FOR THEM TO UNDERSTAND IMMEDIATELY, THEY CAN STILL LEARN.

SOME BELIEVE THAT INFORMATION SHOULD BE LIMITED BECAUSE OF HOW DANGEROUS THE INFORMATION IS. THERE MIGHT HAVE BEEN AN INSTANCE IN THE PAST WHERE A KID GOT AHOLD OF AN OLD MANUSCRIPT AND ACCIDENTALLY OPENED A PORTAL TO ANOTHER DIMENSION, SO STEPS HAVE BEEN TAKEN TO PREVENT THAT FROM HAPPENING AGAIN.

SOME BELIEVE INFORMATION SHOULD BE LIMITED TO PEOPLE BECAUSE AN UNEDUCATED SOCIETY IS EASIER TO CONTROL. THEY MIGHT USE THEIR POSITION TO MANIPULATE HOW MUCH INFORMATION IS GIVEN TO ANOTHER, OR EVEN GIVE FALSE INFORMATION, BECAUSE THE OTHER PERSON CAN'T CONTRADICT IT, AND THEREFORE CAN'T CHALLENGE ITS AUTHORITY.

HOWEVER, SOMETIMES TEXTS ARE LIMITED BECAUSE THERE MIGHT BE VERY FEW OF THEM, OR THE BOOKS ARE EXTREMELY EXPENSIVE, SO THEY'RE ONLY ENTRUSTED TO PEOPLE WHO HAVE PROVEN RESPONSIBLE ENOUGH TO HANDLE THEM WITHOUT DAMAGING THEM. THEY MIGHT ALLOW ACCESS UNDER SPECIFIC CIRCUMSTANCES, BUT OTHERWISE RELY ON OTHER METHODS FOR INFORMATION TO BE SHARED.

____

____

____

____

____

Do people go to school?

It's arguable whether school is necessary or not, but it's not arguable about education being necessary for society. Education is defined as the process of receiving or giving systematic instruction, especially at a school or university, but education can happen from a parent, as part of an apprenticeship program, or even self-study.

When thinking about your world, think about whether school is necessary. For example, a blacksmith teaching a younger person to be a blacksmith is a great way for the person to learn, since they have hands-on training in a place it's actually applicable. A fisherman can learn effectively from expert fishermen out on the boat, and a carpenter can learn best actually building a house.

However, sometimes there are subjects that everyone in society should know, and so there might be more of a classroom setting for said subjects. Our modern society believes everyone should be able to read, write, do math, know history, and understand sciences to a degree, believing that makes for a complete person.

Think about what kind of society exists in your book, whether or not they value school, and whether school is necessary for society to function.

____

____

____

____

____

How do People Learn Their Trade?

In a society where people learn a specific trade, like carpentry or blacksmithing, they're taught the skills by a master of that trade. Often the child will follow in the father's footsteps, so a blacksmith's son may be learning about blacksmithing as soon as they're old enough to hold a hammer. Sometimes a parent will want a better life for their child, however, and will pay the master to take the child as an apprentice.

Sometimes people go to school to learn their trade. If they go to school, is the schooling free, provided by the state, or does it cost money paid by individuals? Is some schooling free while others cost money, and is there some schooling that is more expensive than others?

Sometimes people just answer a "help wanted" sign in the window, and the job provides them training while there.

When thinking about who your character is, and why they do what they do, think also about how they got the training to do it, and if there are other opportunities they would prefer to explore.

____

____

____

____

____

____

How long would it take someone to travel 20 miles?

The average person can walk one mile in twenty minutes. Twenty minutes per mile multiplied by twenty miles gives you 400 minutes, or about 6-7 hours of travel. Factoring in breaks for meals and, you know, that, as well as changes in elevation and terrain, and you're looking at about 8-10 hours.

A horse could make the same distance in about half the time while also carrying the person and all the gear they'll need once they get to their destination.

A car traveling 60 miles per hour will hit 20 miles in about 20 minutes, but a commercial airline will cover that distance in about two.

With this question, think about the technology and transportation systems available to people. Do they use vehicles, animals, or are they limited to their feet? Is the ground flat and clear, or is there elevation and terrain to worry about? Can the average person utilize the fastest method of travel? Are there well-established roads?

____

____

____

____

____

____

____

What kinds of weapons are in your world?

A long time ago… in a galaxy far, far, away, people were using blaster pistols and blaster rifles pretty much constantly. A poor person in possession of a blaster was just seen as the norm, while a sword, especially a laser sword, carried with it more prestige.

In many fantasy settings, though, having a sword was common, and it was almost expected that a person would carry a dagger at the least. Bows were also common, depending on the occupation, but armor was usually more restricted, and reserved for the fighting force.

Societies in our world have developed many different kinds of weapons. These weapons were created based on the needs of the user, the capability of the user, and the resources available, and once different resources became available or depleted, the weapon changed as well.

Think about what resources are available, how people have needed weapons, and what types of weapons would come as a result.

____

____

____

____

____

____

____

Who has access to weapons?

Just because a weapon exists in the world doesn't mean everyone is going to have access to it.

Sometimes weapons are restricted due to people wanting control over another. Sometimes weapons are restricted because there's no one that can produce them, making them rare. Sometimes weapons are restricted because they cost a lot to make, and most people can't afford them. Sometimes weapons are restricted because society won't use a certain kind of weapon.

Whatever the case, in your world, think about who has access to weaponry and whether the average person would even have them. Then think about who knows how to use them, and how training in them is acquired.

____

____

____

____

____

____

____

____

____

____

What languages are spoken?

It's very common for everyone to have a common language in books, because we want our characters to be able to converse with each other. We want our characters to be able to talk to others, buy stuff easily, read the books they come across, but mostly, I think we as the author don't want to create a new language.

However, just like there are many languages in our world, it's perfectly reasonable for there to be multiple languages in a fantasy world. Why wouldn't the elves have their language and dwarves have theirs? Why wouldn't there be different languages that humans speak? It's not unreasonable at all that different races would have different ways of speaking.

When thinking about whether or not there are different languages, consider where those languages would be spoken, who would know them, whether or not people could learn them, and what problems could arise with your character not being able to read or understand a specific language.

____

____

____

____

____

____

____

What kinds of people are honored in your world?

Looking at the kinds of people that are honored gives a good idea of what the people value. Sometimes the people honored in a city are going to be different than those honored at a national, or world level, because some people will matter on a global scale, and some will matter on a much smaller one.

In Lord of the Rings, Tolkien was really good at showing this. There were elves who were renowned for their wisdom and age, fighting prowess, and their crafting ability. The elves, therefore, valued wisdom, combat ability, and crafting. The Hobbits, on the other hand, valued simple things, and the most renowned among them were farmers and gardeners, and warriors were held in lower esteem.

When thinking about important people in your world, think about what you value and the kinds of people you think should be held in esteem.

____

____

____

____

____

____

____

____

Are there dragons in your world?

It almost seems like a fantasy world isn't complete these days without dragons, but that doesn't mean they need to be in your world.

One beauty about dragons is also a major problem: they are constantly depicted differently. In some stories, all dragons are the enemy. In some stories, dragons can be beneficial allies. In some stories dragons are large and powerful. In some stories dragons are small and mischievous.

Whatever your view of dragons, do you even want them in your world? Would another kind of creature work better for the role dragons would play? Did dragons exist at one point in history and they're now extinct? This is your world, so make in it what you feel would be best.

____

____

____

____

____

____

____

____

____

What kinds of supernatural creatures exist in your world?

Dragons aren't the only kinds of creatures at home in a fantasy world. Stories have been filled with magical and supernatural creatures for ages, including faeries, centaurs, trolls, ogres, giants, griffons, and so many more.

Supernatural creatures add to the fantasy, setting clear distinctions between our world and the created world, which allows the reader to immerse themselves easier. They are often similar to other creatures, for example, a Pegasus is a normal horse with wings, or a unicorn is a horse with a single horn. They could also be a combination of two or more animals, like the griffon, chimera, or manticore. Sometimes they're a normal creature that can speak, teleport, glow, or some other fantastic ability.

Although it is perfectly fine not to have any magical creatures in your stories, think about it a little more, because it's not unreasonable in a world touched by magic for the creatures to be touched as well.

____

____

____

____

____

____

____

Is there racism in your world?

Racism doesn't have to exist in your world. What's interesting, though, even though it's called racism, it doesn't really exist in ours either. Racism is a belief that one race is inferior or superior to another. Therefore, in our world, since we all belong to the human race, you can see how the term doesn't make sense.

Racism can develop, however, often for logical reasons. If a war happened between elves and humans and the elves won, that could create a mindset of elf superiority for years. If a dwarven community had an elf that couldn't match them physically, they may believe elves are weaker. If a human community stole something precious to the dwarves, the dwarves may consider humans to be thieves and untrustworthy. Those mindsets will be taught to later generations, and soon, races are naturally prejudiced toward one another.

In your story, think about if there is animosity between different races and whether that appears in your tale or not. Think about if some event may have caused it, and if there are some trying to fight it. Consider, too, a character developing racism because of the actions of one race and how that will affect the story.

____

____

____

____

____

Are men and women considered equal in your world?

There are lots of stories where men are the dominant sex and women are the inferiors. There are many stories where women are superior. There are many stories where men and women are equal. There are also many stories where men and women are different, but they've appreciated the differences in each other.

When designing your world, consider the role gender has in your story and how it affects characters' mindsets. Is the leadership primarily male or female? Are there special male only groups and female only groups, or do groups have to be mixed? Does one gender tend towards certain jobs more than the others, or are all jobs split equally male and female? Is the military primarily one gender or is it split down the middle? Are there more criminals of one gender than another?

____

____

____

____

____

____

____

____

What do people do for leisure?

You always hear you need to find a good work/life balance, but it's amazing how we don't see a lot of leisure activities in books unless it's with children. More often than not, you'll see a person having meals with a family, but the rest of their time is at some occupation or sleeping. This, of course, is not necessarily including the main character, since they're doing whatever quest they're called to.

However, the other characters are people, too, and they're going to have lives outside of the story, so explore that a bit. Explore what a community likes to do, what activities they do together, what games they play. Do they have festivals? Do they have holidays? Do they have places they go to for leisure? Is there any time for leisure at all, or are they literally slaves to a system?

Just like work should not be our whole life, think about your characters.

Are there sports in your world?

Sports are a great way to bring people together. It is enjoyable to see individuals competing at the peak of ability, and supporting a team creates a community of a similar interest, regardless of how different the people are otherwise. Sports can also be a way someone from poverty can move into wealth and in turn bring others up. Sports are also a way to create different classes of people.

In our society, a lot of people enjoy watching sports of some kind, be it basketball, baseball, football, soccer, tennis, hockey, etc. They especially love the excitement of being at a game or watching with others, and your characters might too. Think not only about if there are sports, but what kinds of sports, and how important sports are to society. Are there some sports that people like more than others, or are all sports equal? Is there any benefit to being on a particular team, or do they just play to play? Are there particular stakes on whether or not a team loses, or is it all just for fun?

____

____

____

____

____

____

____

What is the life expectancy of people?

On average, the life expectancy of a person in our world is 69 years for men and 74 years for women. The United States is slightly higher at 73.5 and 79, but Hong Kong is sitting at 83 and 88, while Chad is sitting at 51 and 54. We are all human, so we're all the same race, but where we live greatly affects our access to technology, resources, and medicine.

In a fantasy world, there's also magic that can be used as healing, so the life expectancy of people may actually be higher. Medicines are more local with fewer of them controlled by larger corporations, so the costs may be much cheaper and more accessible. If a doctor didn't have to worry about lawsuits, the entire practice could be considerably cheaper for everyone.

Also, in a fantasy world, some races just live longer than others, so think about what that would affect. Are old people common or rare? If a person lives to 100, is that an oddity, or expected? Has something happened to change life expectancy?

____

____

____

____

____

____

____

What kinds of clothing do people wear?

When you think about what you're wearing right now, ask yourself this: why are you wearing it? Are you wearing what you are for practical reasons, like because it's cold, hot, rainy, or sunny? Are you wearing it for a social reason, like because you're at a formal event or a sports event? Are you wearing it because it's just comfortable, like a favorite sweatshirt or pair of shorts? Now think and ask yourself this: is what you're wearing typical of the people around you?

People are going to dress similarly in a place whether they realize it or not. Sure, there are going to be some outliers, but in general, the colder it is the more clothing they'll wear, and the warmer it is, the less clothing. Think about what kinds of styles the people wear, though. Think about if any colors are common. Think about whether there are different kinds of clothing for different occasions. Think, also, about whether or not dresses have pockets.

____

____

____

____

____

____

____

What kind of music exists in your world?

Music has constantly changed over the years, namely because of the technology available, but also the daring of individuals. When guitars went electric, it caused a lot of controversy, but hundreds of years ago, there was another problem with what were called "Devil's Chords." People have constantly experimented, either with instruments, computers, or just themselves.

Singing is great because it requires no instruments, so if an instrument was not available, singing still was. Piano is great, but not everyone has a piano in their home or even access to one, so those have more limited availability. Reed instruments are great with great sound, but with string instruments you can sing, as well.

When thinking about the music available, try to close your eyes, imagine if your place was shown in a movie, and then imagine what music would be playing. What kinds of instruments are used? Is it fast or slow? Are their lyrics or just notes? Are people dancing or sitting still?

____

____

____

____

____

____

What is the punishment for crime?

Some people believe you just have to tell someone not to do something again, and that's enough to make them change. Some believe a fine should be paid. Some believe a beating is necessary. Some believe jail is best. Some believe in the death penalty.

However, it's rare that you'll find someone who believes the punishment for all crimes should be the same. Most believe the punishment should fit the crime, and if a person ran a red light, it'd be tough to find someone who believes the culprit should get the death penalty.

In your world, think about what kinds of crimes people could commit, and what is preventing them from committing said crimes. Do they live in a world where the slightest infraction is gravely punished, or do they live in a world where no crime is punished? Do people feel safe, or do they always have to keep eyes in the back of their head? Is your character a criminal? Were they a criminal?

____

____

____

____

____

____

____

____

What is considered a large city?

Determining what constitutes a large city is going to come down to you. What one person might consider a large city is what another might consider a small one. For example, a person coming from a small village of one hundred people would consider a city of 100,000 people to be large. However, a person coming from a city of 1,000,000 people would consider that same city to be quite small.

However, if there are no cities larger than 100,000 people, then the city will be large by everyone's standards. Therefore, when you're thinking about cities and towns and villages, think about if there are particular locations where a lot of people would be gathered.

Remember, a large city needs lots of resources to keep the population sustained, so think about things like trade routes, natural resources, agriculture, industry, and whether the land can be easily developed.

____

____

____

____

____

____

____

____

What Is Considered a Large Army?

There's almost something romantic about the idea of millions of troops coming together to fight each other on the battlefield, but those numbers aren't necessarily reasonable. To put it in perspective, when the orcs attacked Helm's Deep in Lord of the Rings: The Two Towers, Saruman said the numbers of orcs were in the tens of thousands. When Gondor was attacked in Return of the King, there were about 12,500 men on Gondor's side, about half of which were brought by Theoden of Rohan, and tens of thousands on Mordor's side.

Looking at our world, the largest military in the world is China at about two million, but this number is only about 0.14% of the total population. Russia's military is about 6% of its population, Canada's military is 0.17% of the population, Great Britain's military is 0.22% of its population, and the United States' military is 0.42% of its population, just to name a few.

When thinking about how large of a force that could be assembled on the battlefield, think also about how many are even in the military, and then go from there. After all, only under the direst circumstances would a nation call upon every soldier to fight a single battle. Most would hold some in reserve.

____

____

____

____

Is slavery legal in your world?

Slavery is a practice that has been done for thousands of years, and only recently have countries started to abolish it. Many parts of the world still practice it in some form.

Slavery wasn't always bad, however. Yes, some slaves were captured combatants, and some slaves were enslaved from their own population, but some slaves were people who sold themselves to pay for debts if they were unable to pay otherwise. Some slaves were willing gladiators who were looking for a better life.

In your world, think about if there are slaves or not, and if there are, consider why someone is a slave. Is slavery a major part of the country, or frowned upon? Are slaves treated well or cruelly? Do slaves have rights or no?

____

____

____

____

____

____

____

____

____

____

What kind of swearing is there in your world?

It's always funny when someone throws an insult, but the other person doesn't understand the insult, and as such doesn't give the rise that was expected. As an American, when I watch British television shows, I often don't catch the swearing because they aren't swear words in my culture, or they may say something that is considered a swear word here that isn't anything bad at all there.

When thinking about your world, are there any words or phrases that people would use to express frustration, pain, insult, and offense? Are there any expressions or words they would use that wouldn't register as bad in your society? How did these words come to be bad?

____

____

____

____

____

____

____

____

____

____

Are there any prophecies in your world?

If there is a "chosen one" there is probably a prophesy or two about them, maybe more. Furthermore, if there are prophesies, there are probably a lot of people who have put their hope or dread in said prophesy and are either trying to make it come to pass or thwart it completely.

Prophecies are great tools to establish the importance of a character or characters, and readers can often empathize with a character whose destiny is already determined, since they often feel they don't have as much agency in their own story. As a writer, it's an effective way to force characters to do what you want, because otherwise the world will end if they don't.

That being said, since prophecies can have the effect of removing agency from the characters, readers can get bored easier since they know exactly where the story has to and will go. For that reason, a lot of prophecies are vaguer in their wording, as the reader now might know what will happen without knowing how.

That being said, even if you have a prophecy, it doesn't have to be correct, so have fun.

____

____

____

____

____

WHAT DO THE PEOPLE IN YOUR WORLD KNOW ABOUT ITS HISTORY?

IN LORD OF THE RINGS, IT'S OFTEN MENTIONED HOW EVERY ELF KNOWS THE HISTORY OF THEIR WORLD, AND THERE ARE MANY SCENES OF ELVES TELLING STORIES FROM THEIR HISTORY. SOME OF THE ELVES ARE LEARNED IN HISTORY ALL THE WAY BACK TO THE FORMING OF THE WORLD. IN COMPARISON, THERE ARE MANY PEOPLE TODAY WHO DON'T KNOW MUCH HISTORY AT ALL, AND THE ONLY HISTORY THEY KNOW IS ENOUGH TO CLAIM SOME INJUSTICE.

IT'S SAID THAT THOSE WHO FORGET HISTORY ARE DESTINED TO REPEAT IT, SO IN YOUR WORLD, DO PEOPLE REMEMBER THEIR HISTORY? ON THAT NOTE, DO THEY REMEMBER ALL THEIR HISTORY, OR ARE SOME PARTS LEFT OUT? DO THEY KNOW A WRONG HISTORY, OR HAVE THEIR HISTORIANS BEEN ACCURATE? DO THEY BELIEVE THEIR HISTORY? DO THEY WANT TO BELIEVE THEIR HISTORY?

Where do people find hope?

Hope is precious. Hope can keep you going, no matter how dark things feel. Hope can give you strength when strength seems to have left. Hope can give courage when fear threatens to overwhelm. Hope is powerful, and sometimes, hope is the only thing that can keep a character moving forward.

When you think about your own life, think about what gives you hope. Is it a person? Is it a promise? Is it God? Is it a dream? Now think about your world. Do your people have hope in a person or a group of people? Do they have hope in a prophecy? Do they have hope in a power or object they need to find? Or do they have hope in something else entirely?

____

____

____

____

____

____

____

____

____

____

____

Antagonist

WHO IS THE MAIN ANTAGONIST?

ANTAGONISTS CAN COME IN MANY FORMS. SOMETIMES, THEY'RE A VILLAIN, LIKE A DARK LORD WHO IS EVIL FOR EVIL'S SAKE, OR A CHARACTER WHO BECAME EVIL BECAUSE OF OTHER EVENTS. SOMETIMES THEY'RE NOT A VILLAIN, JUST ANOTHER CHARACTER WHO IS IN THE PROTAGONIST'S WAY, AND COULD EVEN BE A BEST FRIEND COMPETING FOR SIMILAR GOALS. SOMETIMES IT'S NATURE, SO EITHER THE ELEMENTS, SOME ANIMAL, OR TIME. SOMETIMES IT'S THE MAIN CHARACTER, AND THE INTERNAL STRUGGLE THEY FACE.

AN ANTAGONIST IS JUST A CHARACTER WHO OPPOSES THE PROTAGONIST, OR THE MAIN CHARACTER, SO STORIES CAN HAVE MULTIPLE ANTAGONISTS. A VILLAIN IS A CHARACTER WHO IS MOTIVATED BY EVIL. OFTEN THE ANTAGONIST IS A VILLAIN, BECAUSE IT'S EASIER TO DISLIKE AN EVIL CHARACTER IF OUR PROTAGONIST IS GOOD, BUT SOMETIMES THE PROTAGONIST ISN'T GOOD AT ALL.

WHEN THINKING ABOUT YOUR ANTAGONIST, THINK ABOUT WHAT GOAL OF THE PROTAGONIST THEY'RE TRYING TO STOP, OR WHAT GOAL OF THEIRS THE PROTAGONIST WANTS TO STOP.

What is your main antagonist's motivation?

An antagonist needs a reason to oppose the protagonist, because otherwise they're not an antagonist. A classing evil villain motivation is trying to take over the world, and the hero doesn't want them to because they don't want evil everywhere. This makes sense, which is why it's commonly used. However, maybe there's something the protagonist did in order to make the antagonist want to do what they are. For example, maybe the protagonist defeated the antagonist's father, so now they're opposing them for revenge.

When you're creating your antagonist, think about what their reason is for doing what they do. Are they just evil, and so they hate good? Were they betrayed by someone close to them? Are they trying to right a wrong? Do they have a bigger plan and this event is just a first step of that plan?

____

____

____

____

____

____

____

____

____

____

What Kind of Being Is Your Main Antagonist?

A lot of people like to use either a demon or demon-like forces for their antagonist, because it's easy to hate evil. Not every dark lord is going to be this obvious, however.

When thinking about your antagonist, think about their race, but also think about other aspects. Are they old or young? Are they male or female? Are they large or small?

Now think about them in terms of your protagonist. Are they similar to your protagonist, or completely different? Are they the same kind of being as your protagonist or different? Same gender or different? Remember, not only are you creating them as their own character, but they also exist because of the protagonist.

____

____

____

____

____

____

____

____

____

____

Does your main antagonist wield supernatural powers?

When you have magic in a book, it's not unreasonable to think the main antagonist might have some form of magic as well. After all, think about these rivalries. Magneto and Professor X. Aragorn and Sauron. Luke Skywalker and Darth Vader. Harry Potter and Voldemort. Naruto and Sasuke. It makes sense, though. We want our villains to feel powerful, so giving them actual powers is an easy way to do that.

When thinking about your antagonist, think about the role magic has in your world and whether it's common or rare. Think about if they do have power and what they did to acquire it. Is there a being they made a deal with? Did they get it through study? Were they born with it?

____

____

____

____

____

____

____

____

____

What are your main antagonist's strengths?

Your main antagonist may be the worst creature imaginable... but there are still things they're good at. This could be the obvious, like they're incredibly strong, or they're a powerful magic user, or they're unbelievably charismatic, but it could be smaller things, like they're loyal to their followers, or they're really cool under pressure.

When thinking about your antagonist, it's very easy to want them to be the opposite of your main character, or it's easy to want them to be weak so the protagonist can defeat them. I would instead think of them as the end goal, so the protagonist has to rise to meet them. If the protagonist can defeat the final boss as a base character, then there's really no point in having a story. On the other hand, if the protagonist has to rise to meet them, then the reader gets to follow the protagonist's struggle, and therefore cares more about seeing them achieve their goal.

____

____

____

____

____

____

____

What are your main antagonist's weaknesses?

Just like a main character needs flaws, an antagonist needs flaws and weaknesses. Flaws can come in many forms, including being physically weak, being unintelligent, being clumsy, or having an allergy. Depending on the situation, it could be that they're too old or too young. It could be that they're obese or too thin. It could also include being cruel, being racist, being obsessed about something to the point of ignoring everything else around them, or not caring at all.

When thinking about the flaws and weaknesses of your antagonist, think about how you want the reader to feel about them. Do you want the reader to empathize with them or hate them? Do you want the reader to laugh at them or be scared of them?

____

____

____

____

____

____

____

____

____

Do people know about your main antagonist?

This sounds strange, but do people actually know about your main antagonist? Now, I don't mean absolutely no one, though that would be an interesting story. I'm talking about the average person. For example, in Star Wars, everyone knows of the Emperor, but the average citizen won't know of Darth Vader, and hardly anyone will have heard of Mara Jade. In Lord of the Rings, despite how big Sauron is and how his plans are for the entire world, most of the hobbits had never heard of him.

In your world, your main antagonist exists for the story, but how big are they in the world in general? Do they oppose many people, or just a few? Do their plans involve the world, or just a small area? Also, do people know of them as a person but don't know of them as an antagonist?

Does your antagonist prefer law and order or chaos?

Oddly, the idea of ruling the world by itself is not evil. You'd have everyone united under a single government, following equally understood laws and codes, and you could bring all people together under a singular goal. Granted, most evil dictators also want to enslave people and take away personal freedoms, but at least things are orderly.

When thinking about your antagonist, ask yourself this. Do they want things to be orderly, or do they want chaos to reign? Are they trying to build something or tear down something? Are they trying to establish a leader or tear down a leader?

Why do people follow your antagonist?

Just because a person is evil doesn't mean they aren't good to their followers. Darth Vader valued efficiency, and when people were good at what they did, he rewarded them for it. Grand Admiral Thrawn was one of the most loved Imperial officers because he rewarded his people when they showed creativity and ingenuity even when the plan failed. Sauron, for all his plans to cover the world in darkness, actually tried to create a place for his orcs to live and prosper.

When thinking about your antagonist, think about why someone would want to follow them? What are they offering other than not killing them? Are they offering them land? Are they offering them power? Are they offering wealth? Are they offering position? Are they offering friendship?

What kinds of people or beings follow your antagonist?

Sauron commanded legions of orcs, but those were not the only beings who followed him. There were also men from the south, trolls, goblins, wargs, and the ring wraiths. He was able to sway Saruman, one of the wisest beings in all of Middle Earth, and he had spies even up in Bree.

Some antagonists are going to command many people, while some are going to lead only a few. When you think about your world and who all is in it, ask yourself what kinds of people would ally themselves with your antagonist. Are they thieves? Assassins? Warriors? Nobles? Commoners? Mages? Hunters? Farmers?

What Is Your Antagonist's Desired Outcome?

We all know the classic story of how the villain wants to take over the world... but what comes after that? Let's say they take over the world. To what end?

When thinking about your antagonist, they're going to have some goal they want to achieve, but what comes after that? What world do they want to create as a result of achieving their goal? The movie Megamind is actually perfect for this, because very quickly into the movie, the villain achieves his goal of defeating the hero, taking over the city... and then he gets bored. Through various events, he realizes he never wanted to actually take over the city, but just wanted a place to belong.

So, what does your antagonist really want?

____

____

____

____

____

____

____

____

____

____

ARE POWERS INHERENTLY GOOD OR EVIL, OR DO THEY DEPEND ON HOW THEY'RE USED?

If you're familiar with Star Wars, you're familiar with the Force, or the energy field created by all living things that surrounds us, penetrates us, and binds the galaxy together. The Force has a dark and a light side, and some abilities are dark by their nature.

In many stories, though, there are mages who are good and mages who are evil, but who use the same kinds of power. How does that work in your world? Are there powers that have an alignment, or are all powers fair game? Are there powers that by using you become evil or cursed? Are there powers that you cannot access unless you are good or evil?

Does Your Antagonist Prefer Beauty or Ugliness?

There's a common trop that when characters are depicted, the more good a character is, the more aesthetically pleasing their appearance, the nicer looking their setting, and the more white their color scheme is. On the other hand, the more evil a character is, the uglier or more sinister everything is... and their color scheme is mostly black.

There's a logical reason for this, though. In comparing good and evil, making them clear opposites of each other helps the reader to be able to distinguish them, and when that image comes up, it will immediately put an image in the reader's head, as well as create immediate emotions.

However, some villains love to dress well and love to surround themselves with beauty. They might be obsessed with beauty to the point that they want to hoard all the beauty for themselves. So, think about your antagonist. Do they appreciate beauty? Do they like to surround themselves with beauty? Do they despise beauty and want to destroy it?

____

____

____

____

____

____

____

Who does your antagonist care about?

Very rarely is it the case where a person does not care about anyone in some way. Darth Vader cared about Padme. Magneto cared about Mystique. Biff Tannen cared about Lorraine. Thanos cared about Gamora. Loki cared about his mother. Even Voldemort cared about Bellatrix.

Now, with a lot of these, you may be thinking this isn't quite accurate. Afterall, we know Voldemort did not love Bellatrix despite her having feelings for him, but he did value her servitude, so in that sense, she was important to him.

Think about this when thinking about your antagonist. Think about who they would care for and why they would care about them. What are they to your antagonist? Also, think about the protagonist. Why does your antagonist care about them?

____

____

____

____

____

____

____

____

____

What Does Your Antagonist Care About?

We've talked about the who the antagonist cares about, so now let's talk about what your antagonist cares about. This one is going to be easier to think about, because at the least, the antagonist is going to have some goal.

Most antagonists are going to care about their own survival, so if that is their main goal, consider looking into deeper motivations. For example, Agent Smith from The Matrix wanted to preserve his own programming at the exclusion of everything else. Sauron wanted the ring to be complete and wanted a place for his people to live. Even Mr. Waternoose from Monsters, Inc was trying to solve a power deficiency problem affecting countless monster lives just trying to survive.

The what could also be a physical thing, like land or money. It could be something earned like a title or prestige. Whatever it is that your antagonist cares about, think about it and use it to shape their motivations.

____

____

____

____

____

____

____

Is there only one main antagonist or are there multiple smaller ones?

This has to do with the world as a whole, because while a character may have just one antagonist they're focused on, there could be many more. When you think about Star Wars, Darth Vader is the main antagonist for Luke, but there's also the Emperor, and the temptation of the dark side of the force. Furthermore, below Darth Vader are all the minions and stormtroopers that come against him.

When thinking about your story, think about the world as a whole and think about if there is a greater story going on.... Not just this book. Are there going to be multiple antagonists throughout the story, or will the story focus on just one?

____

____

____

____

____

____

____

____

____

____

Is there an antagonist greater than the main antagonist?

Many stories will have a personal antagonist, but then they'll also have an antagonist who's even greater or more powerful, possibly even the personal antagonist's master. The Emperor was the master of Darth Vader. Morgoth was the master of Sauron.

Having an antagonist who is more powerful than the primary antagonist is a great way to continue a protagonist's journey to save whatever they're trying to save. After all, if the antagonist is defeated and then there are no more antagonists, then there's not much more story left.

When thinking about your world, think also if you want anything to happen after, or if the world is just done after the antagonist is stopped.

Does good always triumph or does evil win as well?

Whether or not good wins in the end, do they win every battle or is evil allowed to win some as well? It's always exciting to see the protagonist accomplish their goal, especially if it looks like the antagonist might win, but is it realistic that they always win?

Especially if you're writing a series, consider letting the protagonist lose from time to time. If they lose, then the antagonist will feel more threatening and more of a challenge to the reader. In the Karate Kid, for example, Daniel loses pretty much constantly to Johhny, making his final victory much bigger than if he had constantly beat him (and yes, apparently that kick was legal, it was just punches to the face that were illegal).

When thinking about your own story, think about the tone, think about the steaks, and think about how strong your antagonist actually is.

____

____

____

____

____

____

____

____

Are creatures destined to be good or evil, or do they have a choice?

When you think about evil creatures, what comes to mind? Got that image in your head? Perfect. Why are they evil? Are they evil because of the choices they've made? Were they created to be evil? Were they created evil?

When a creature is always evil, then you don't have to think about whether they'll choose to be good or not. They can be attacked and defeated without remorse because the elimination of evil benefits everyone. Dark Lords often take these kinds of beings as their underlings, like the orcs and goblins in Lord of the Rings, the trollocs from Wheel of Time, and almost every instance of zombie or undead.

When thinking about your world and the creatures in it, ask yourself if there are evil creatures, and if so, why are they evil?

____

____

____

____

____

____

____

____

Where does the antagonist live relative to the protagonist?

Sometimes the antagonist lives thousands of miles away, and it's an epic journey just to get to them. Sometimes they're just right out the front door, and they've tormented your protagonist their entire life.

Whatever you decide is going to affect not just the main character, but all the people around them. If the antagonist is only an antagonist for the main character and they live close by, then people will have seen them fight, but if they're an antagonist to everyone, then the main character will likely have many allies. On the other hand, if the antagonist lives far away, then other people either won't have heard of them, or they just don't care.

____

____

____

____

____

____

____

____

____

How do your Characters respond?

A YOUNG LORD THROWS YOUR MC'S BROTHER INTO PRISON. HOW DOES YOUR MC REACT?

YOUR MAIN CHARACTER NEEDS TO BE ALONE. WHO
LOOKS FOR AND FINDS HIM?

Your MC has fallen in battle. There is a sword, an axe, a hammer, a spear, and a bow in front of their best friend. Which do they pick up?

Your main character's sibling has a pet. What kind, and what is its name?

YOUR MAIN CHARACTER DISCOVERS AN ISLAND. WHAT ARE THEY CALLING IT?

A GEM CHANGES COLOR BASED ON THE PERSON HOLDING IT. YOUR MC'S BEST FRIEND GRABS IT, AND IT ACTUALLY GLOWS BRIGHTLY. WHAT COLOR IS IT?

A princess gives your MC an object wrapped in rags. How does your MC respond?

Your MC dies. How do they die?

Your MC is trying to rally their friends. What do they say?

ONE HUNDRED YEARS INTO THE FUTURE, A BARD BEGINS THE SONG OF YOUR CHARACTER'S ADVENTURES. WHAT ARE THE LYRICS?

When your MC dies, who speaks at the memorial
and what do they say?

What is the last thing your MC says?

50 STORY IDEAS TO GET YOUR MIND GOING.

1. While sleeping, a young boy dreams of teleporting to another world. When they wake up, they find they've actually traveled there.

2. A new student arrives at your class knowing a language that doesn't exist on earth.

3. One day after accidentally cutting herself, a young teen notices her blood turns silver.

4. The first time an old farmer picks up a sword it says, "thank you."

5. A band of raiders invades your village, but for some reason cannot see you.

6. A TAILOR FINDS A CHEST BRANDED WITH A CREST FROM A LONG DEAD EMPIRE BURIED IN THEIR ATTIC.

7. EVERY TIME AN OLD BLACKSMITH THROWS AN OBJECT, IT APPEARS BACK IN THEIR HAND MOMENTS LATER.

8. ON THEIR THIRTEENTH BIRTHDAY, A YOUNG GIRL UNDERSTANDS WHAT HER DOG MEANS WHEN THEY BARK.

9. A WIDOW DISCOVERS HER WEDDING RING GLOWS WHEN SOMEONE TELLS A LIE.

10. YOUR CHILDHOOD TEDDY BEAR GETS UP FROM THE CORNER AND HUGS YOU WHEN YOU'RE SAD ONE DAY.

11. THE MOST POPULAR KID IN SCHOOL FINDS A JOURNAL IN THEIR BASEMENT TALKING ABOUT

12. WHEN AN OLD WATCH MAKER ADJUSTS A
CLIENT'S WATCH, HE FINDS TIME GOES
FORWARD OR REVERSES AS MUCH AS HE MOVES
THE HANDS.

13. WHEN OUT FISHING, A POOR FISHERMAN
ACCIDENTALLY CATCHES A PREHISTORIC
CREATURE.

14. A PRINCESS LEARNS THEIR MOTHER IS
ACTUALLY A DRAGON.

15. A YOUTUBE CHANNEL HAS BEEN DISCOVERED
THAT PREDICTS THE FUTURE EXACTLY THREE
MONTHS IN ADVANCE. TWO AND A HALF
MONTHS AGO IT SHUTS DOWN, WITH THE LAST

VIDEO BEING A VOICE THAT SAYS, "I'M SO
SORRY."

16. YOU PUT ON A RING YOU FOUND IN AN OLD
SHOP AND HEAR THE WORDS, "THIS ONE MAKES
EIGHT, ONLY ONE TO GO," ECHO IN YOUR
HEAD.

17. THE TEMPERATURE GETS COLDER WHEN ONE
BOY GETS SAD AND HOTTER WHEN HIS SISTER
GETS ANGRY.

18. YOU TRAVEL ACROSS COUNTRY FOR THE FIRST
TIME, AND WHEN YOU ARRIVE AT YOUR
DESTINATION, EVERYONE GREETS YOU LIKE AN
OLD FRIEND, KNOWING DETAILS ABOUT
YOURSELF YOU'VE NEVER TOLD ANYONE.

19. COFFEE GIVES SOME PEOPLE ACTUAL SUPER
POWERS.

20. For one day a year, you succeed at anything you attempt, and for one day a year, you just can't do anything right. You never know when those days are, however.

21. Every year on one man's birthday, he forgets the past week and can never recall it after.

22. When a young girl gazes into a lake, the reflection is not hers, and it speaks to her.

23. Your best friend hands you a book, whispers, "goodbye," and then disappears before your eyes. When you open the book, you see their name after a long list of others.

24. An elf walks up to you, bows, and addresses you as nobility.

25. You're reading a book and discover everything that happens to the main character eventually happens to you. The good news is there are four other sequels. The bad news is that book 6 was stopped halfway through.

26. A young farmer discovers that the dark lord that died a thousand years ago is his dad... and not actually dead.

27. You find out the person you have a crush on is being hunted by a dark wizard.

28. After an eclipse, it's discovered that people around the world have forgotten random details about events or items existing.

29. You wake up in the world of the last fantasy book you're reading and see a book on the nightstand about the world you left.

30. A YOUNG LORD CRASHES ON YOUR SHORE AND HAS DAYS TO LIVE UNLESS SOMETHING IS DONE.

31. THE CREATURES FROM YOUR NIGHTMARES AMBUSH AND KILL YOUR PATROL, BUT YOU'RE THE ONLY ONE LEFT.

32. YOU FIND A KNIFE THAT CAN CUT THROUGH ANYTHING, INCLUDING THE FABRIC OF REALITY.

33. LIGHTNING HITS YOU, AND NOW YOU CAN SEE SOUNDS AND HEAR COLORS.

34. ON YOUR TWENTIETH BIRTHDAY, WORDS FLASH IN THE SKY SAYING, "TUTORIAL COMPLETED."

35. A MAN FINDS HIS CELL PHONE CAN CONTACT PEOPLE WHO HAVE DIED.

36. In a world that only tells the truth, one man learns to lie.

37. Everything you write comes true.

38. You discover a cave where the deeper in you go, the younger you become.

39. An old wizard tells you you're going on an adventure.

40. The man your uncle said killed your father is actually your real father.

41. When you utter the words of an ancient language, strange things happen.

42. A group of kids discover their closet door opens into a whole new world.

43. In an instance, half of the people you know disappear.

44.   After a world war, villages try to pick up the pieces and start anew.

45. You have the chance to destroy your enemy completely with the push of a button, saving countless civilizations, but in the process, you destroy your own people... save for yourself.

46. An old man sees your small, crescent-shaped birthmark, and with tears in his eyes, joyfully says, "at last, I've found you."

47.   An old man sees your small, crescent-shaped birthmark, and with a wicked grin exclaims, "at last, I've found you."

48. Your father, the king, remarries, and his new wife wants you dead.

49. Weapons have been outlawed for hundreds of years. On your eighteenth birthday, your father pulls out a sword, hands it to you, and says, "It is time."

50. Three old women can predict the future with perfect accuracy. You make a game out of doing something else.

How to Create a Fantasy Map

Maps are often a staple in fantasy novels, mainly because fantasy novels take place somewhere other than our world. Having a map gives the reader an immediate view of the world, and often serves as a way to get their bearings with what is happening and makes the reader dream about what is in the rest of the world. Fantasy maps are equally useful for authors in keeping things organized, but it also gives the author the chance to dream about what else is in their world, which hopefully gives them more story ideas.

The important thing to remember about creating a map, however, is that there is no one right way. You have the Lord of the Rings style, Game of Thrones style, Redwall style, Wheel of Time style, and a great many more that are unbelievably fantastic. However, I have seen many wrong ways, many boring ways, and while I won't be mentioning them specifically, I know some probably popped into your head when you read this.

Part of showing you how I create my maps for my books will also be explaining why I'm doing it that way. Some reasons will be

PRACTICAL, AND OTHERS WILL BE ARTISTIC. OTHER REASONS WILL BE BECAUSE OF THE TECHNOLOGY USED, WHETHER IT BE ON THE COMPUTER, OR WHETHER IT BE PEN AND PAPER. MY FIRST MAPS WERE PENCIL, PAPER, AND PEN, AND AS AN ARTIST, THEY'RE STILL MY FAVORITE WAY TO CREATE.

I'M ALSO GOING TO GET INTO A COUPLE ELEMENTS, NAMELY MOUNTAINS AND FORESTS. THERE ARE SO MANY WAYS TO DEPICT MOUNTAINS AND MOUNTAIN RANGES, SO WHILE I'M ONLY PROVIDING THREE OF THEM, THEY'RE THE THREE THAT I USE AND AM COMFORTABLE SHOWING. IN THE SAME WAY, WHILE OTHERS HAVE MANY STYLES FOR FORESTS, I only use a couple, and I like to keep it simple.

Alright, then, I think that's it. Let's do it.

First, allow me to welcome you to our fantasy nation of Kennalara. This particular landmass is in the northern hemisphere of our world, around the 45 - 60 degree mark if we're being technical. There are six smaller countries inside it, named Duagwyn, Glas, Aelain, Faclan, Kust, and Sari, and each have their own culture and customs. However, right now, we are not going to get into that. That is a task for another day. For you see, this world starts as...

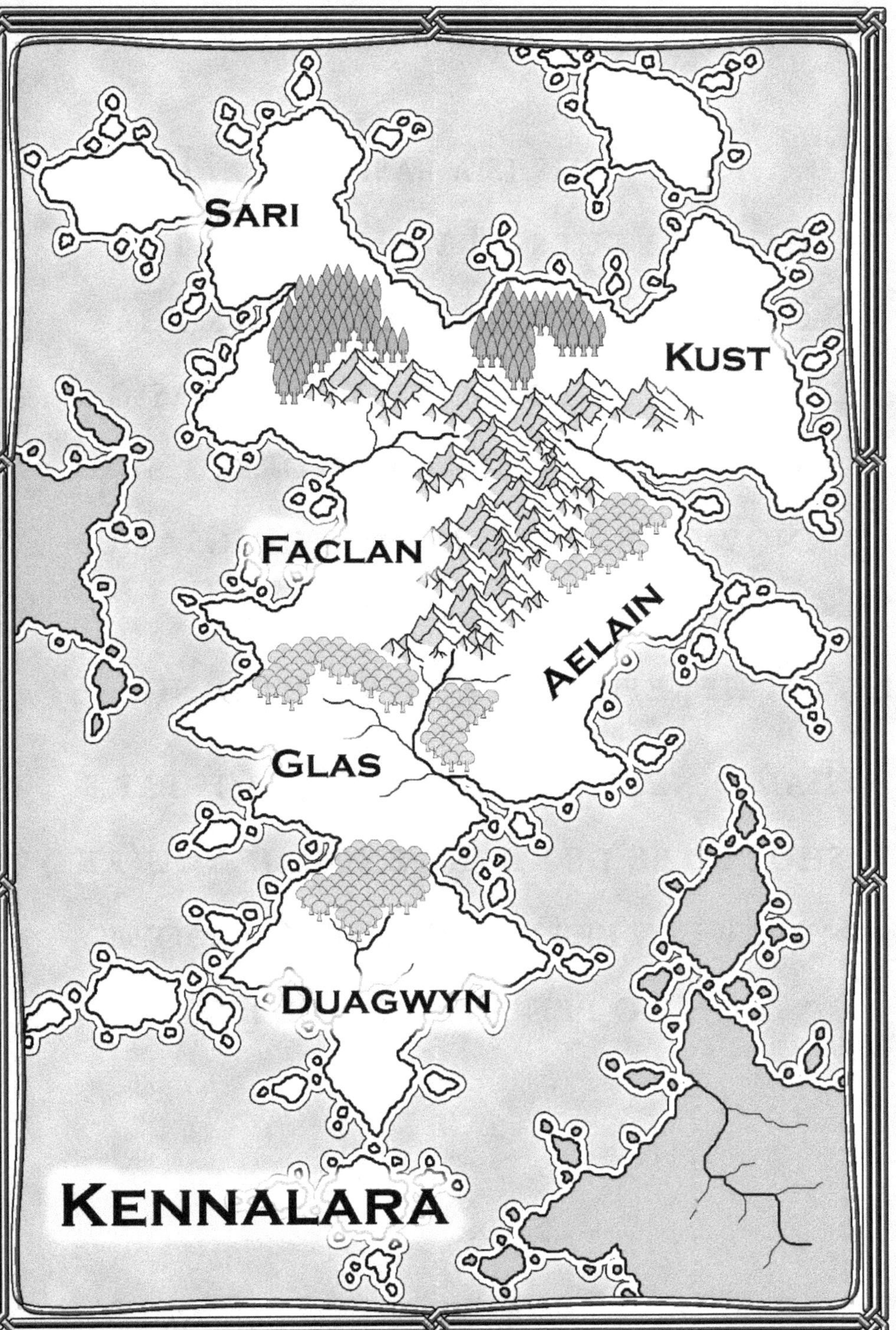

SARI
KUST
FACLAN
AELAIN
GLAS
DUAGWYN
KENNALARA

... THIS. THIS IS A BASIC BLOB. IF I HAVE TO GUESS, I WOULD SAY THAT YOU HAVE PROBABLY SEEN MAPS THAT ARE SOMETHING LIKE THIS, A BASIC BLOB, AND WHILE IT CAN WORK, I ALSO KNOW THERE ARE MORE THINGS YOU CAN DO TO MAKE IT BETTER. THEREFORE, WE'LL KEEP GOING.

I ALSO NEED TO ADD HERE, THIS PART SHOULD BE DONE IN PENCIL IF YOU'RE DRAWING IT BY HAND. WE'LL MOVE ON TO PEN IN A LITTLE BIT.

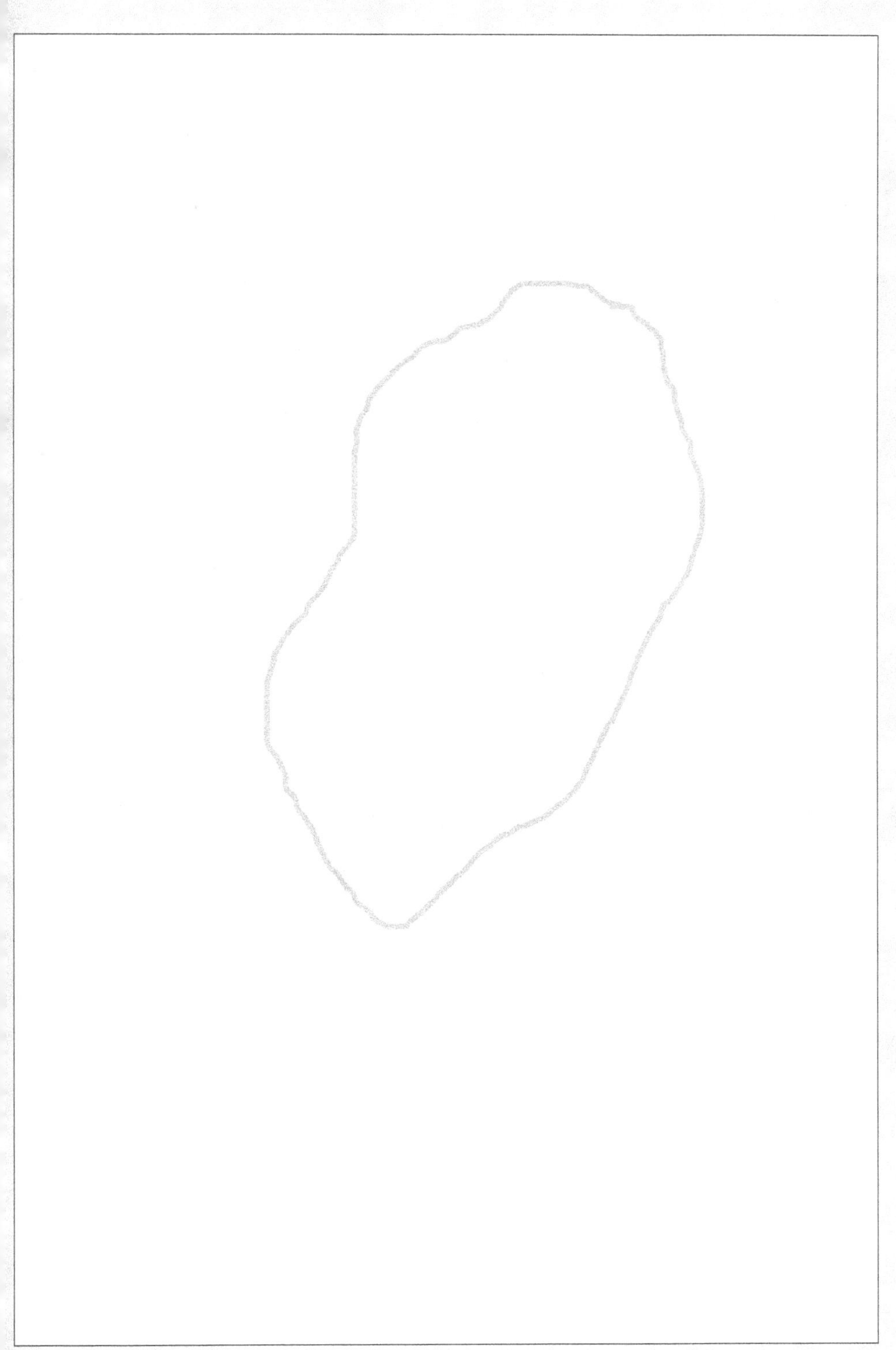

In this step, I'm adding on to what we already had by drawing in a few extra chunks on our main land. I could be technical by saying I'm drawing in peninsulas, but I hesitate to use that term, since I'm going to be doing stuff to them later.

Even though this is in pencil, don't worry about erasing yet. There will be a time where it'll make more sense, and erasing now is just an unnecessary step.

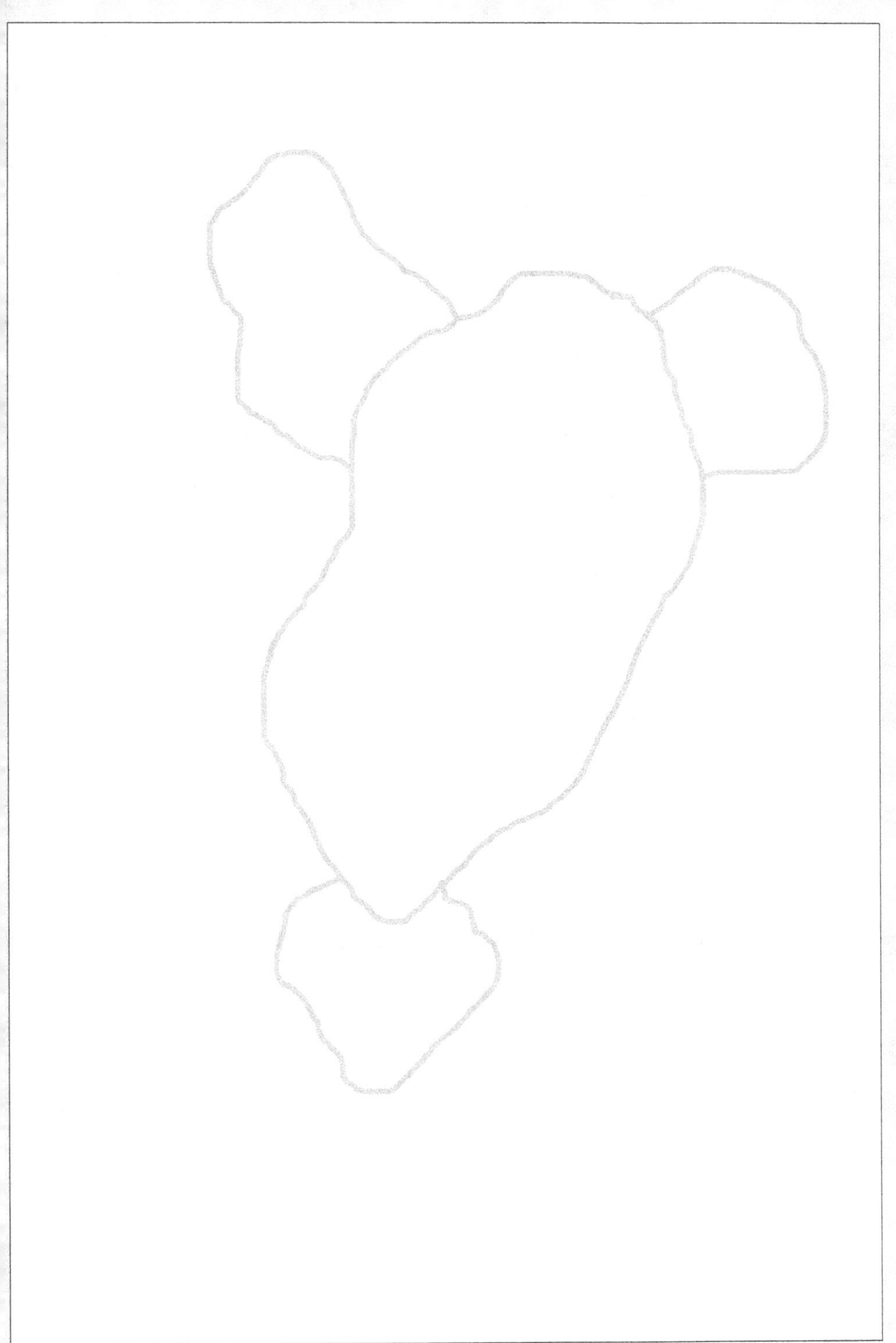

Here you'll notice that all I added were a couple land masses off to the side and in the bottom corner. When I do my maps, I like having my land go to the edge of the map, because it tells me that there is more map to be explored. It gives the impression that the world is far bigger than the little snapshot we're given right here... regardless of whether said world has been created or not. The reader doesn't need to know if it's not.

Now I add peninsulas on our peninsulas, which gives our little land a bit of character. I also went in and added some major bays. Bays are good because we know that's where rivers run into, so marking larger bays in the early stages helps us to plan out our major rivers and lakes.

From an art standpoint, we're also blending the positive and negative space. Finding a balance between the two makes the map aesthetically pleasing.

In this stage, I've gone over our coastline with a darker color, so this is the point you'd go over it with a black pen. I also do, what I call, muddying up the coastline. Basically, I just try to avoid using prefect lines, and just dance my pen back and forth over the guide lines. This is because in the real world, very rarely are natural coastlines perfect lines, there's usually some wiggle. This alone will add a sense of realism.

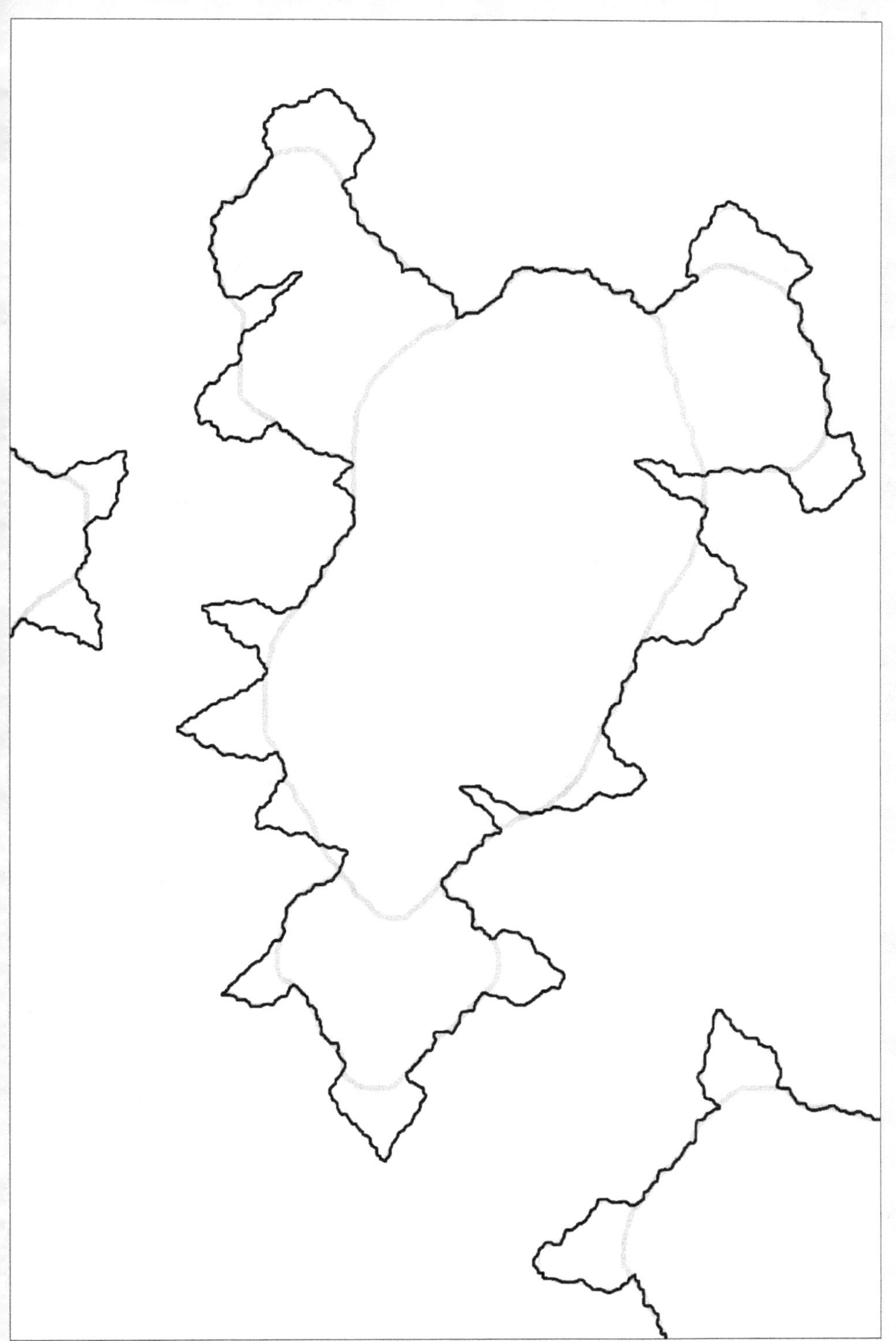

In this next step I erased the guide lines. Yes, now is that time. As we can see, this end result is pretty close to what we end up with… and it all started with that basic blob. Important note, don't erase right after you go over it in pen, as the ink will streak. Blow on it and wait a few minutes for it to dry.

You could stop here, keep the land mass as it is, and your map will be pretty sweet. However, I'm going to keep going, and then get into…

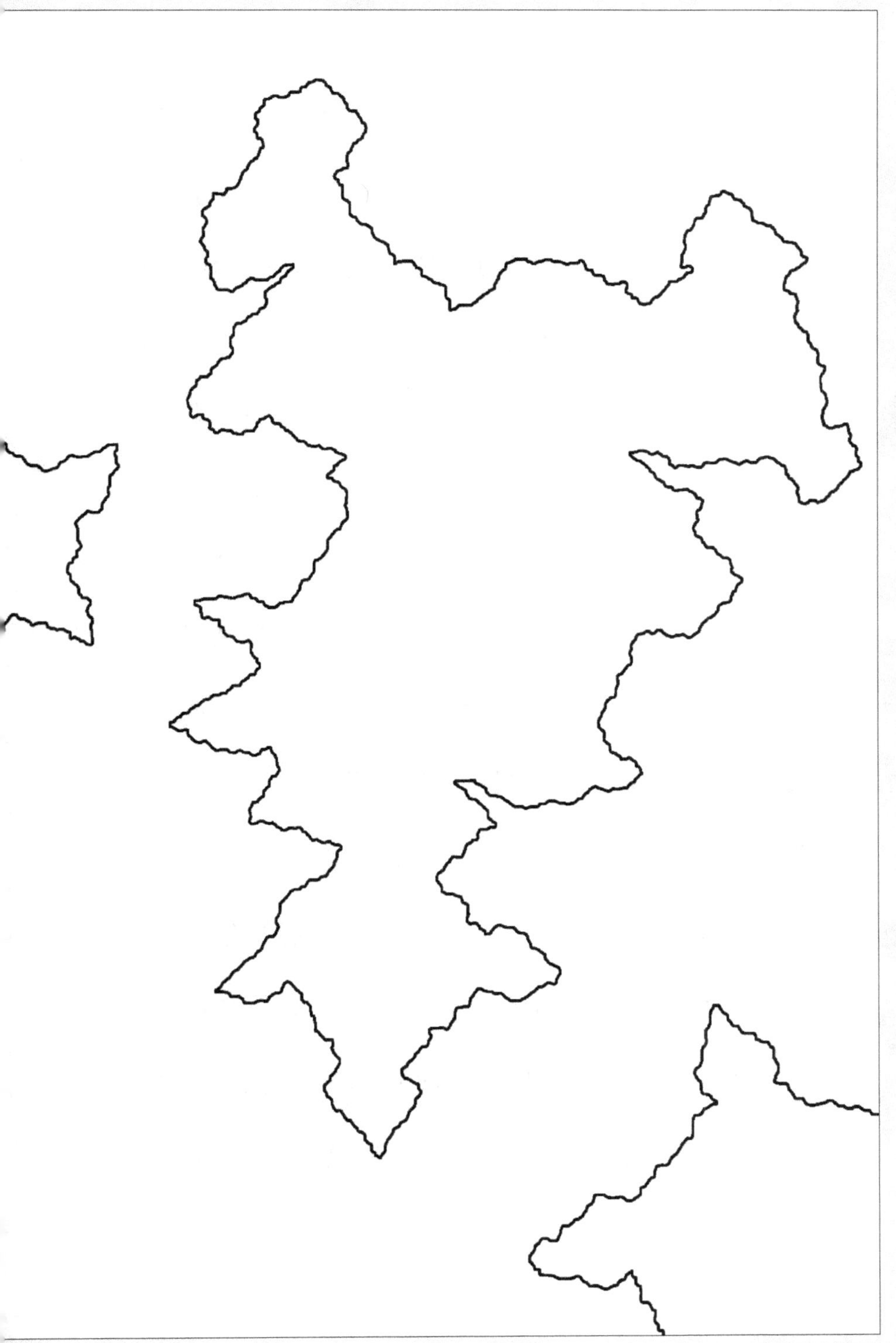

Islands. Islands are another great way to use up negative space. I like to work in stages, putting the big islands in at once and then moving towards the smaller ones, but you can add them at whatever stage. The idea is that likely, due to plate tectonics, chunks of land will break away from others, so I try to place islands in what seems reasonable. I'm not taking hot spots (like Hawaii) into consideration on this one, but in your map, please feel free.

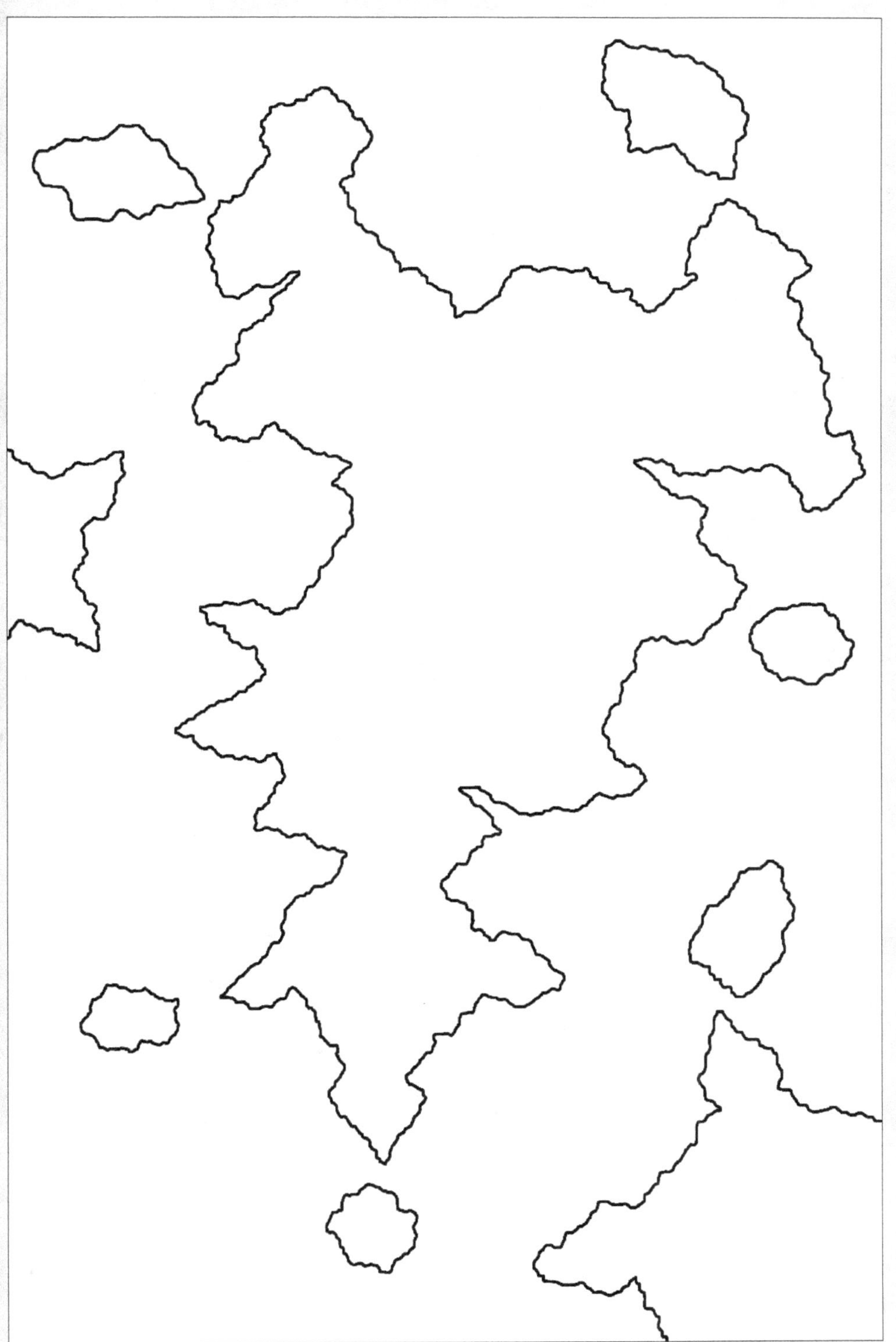

After the big islands I move on to the smaller islands. These islands are likely pieces broken off from the main land or from the larger islands, or it's possible that they're just mountains that would connect to the larger land mass if tides were different. Regardless, I often include small islands in between larger islands to take the breakage into account. I also add smaller islands at the ends of peninsulas, as if it were a piece of the peninsula that had broken off.

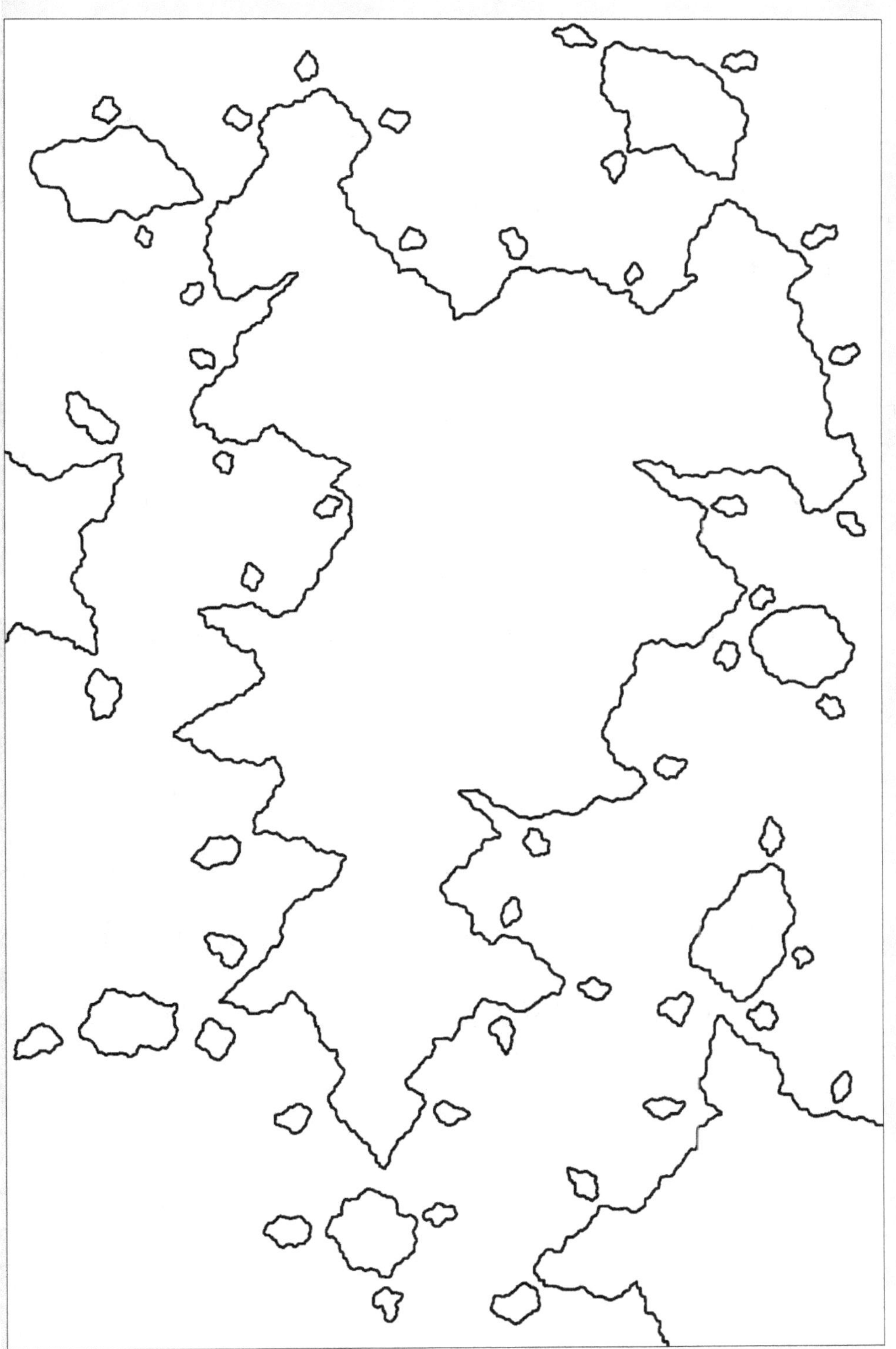

After the smaller islands... come even smaller islands, and these little guys are great for filling in little gaps as well as giving the coast, and even some islands, a little character. Often in the real world, we see islands in clusters or groups, islands like Hawaii, or off in Washington. For me, I grew up in Alaska, and we have many islands and small islands communities, so including multiple islands just comes naturally. Plus, I really like the look.

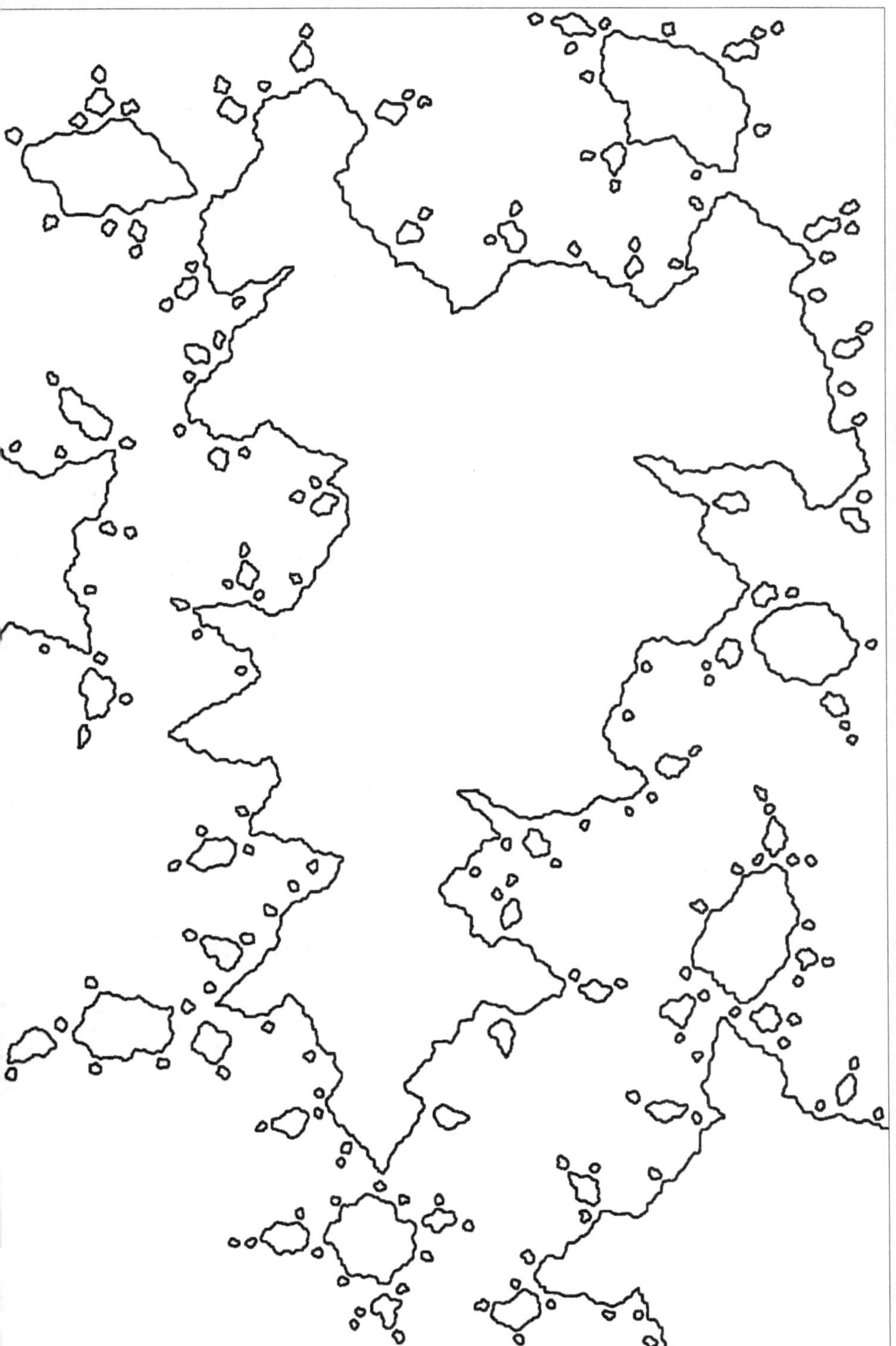

The next stage is to color the water. While this stage is optional (I've seen many maps that are only black and white lines with no gray), I like coloring in the water, so it gives a clear distinction of which is which. This also plays into the negative space I was talking about, because the gray balances out the white, which is something the human eye picks up on without necessarily realizing it.

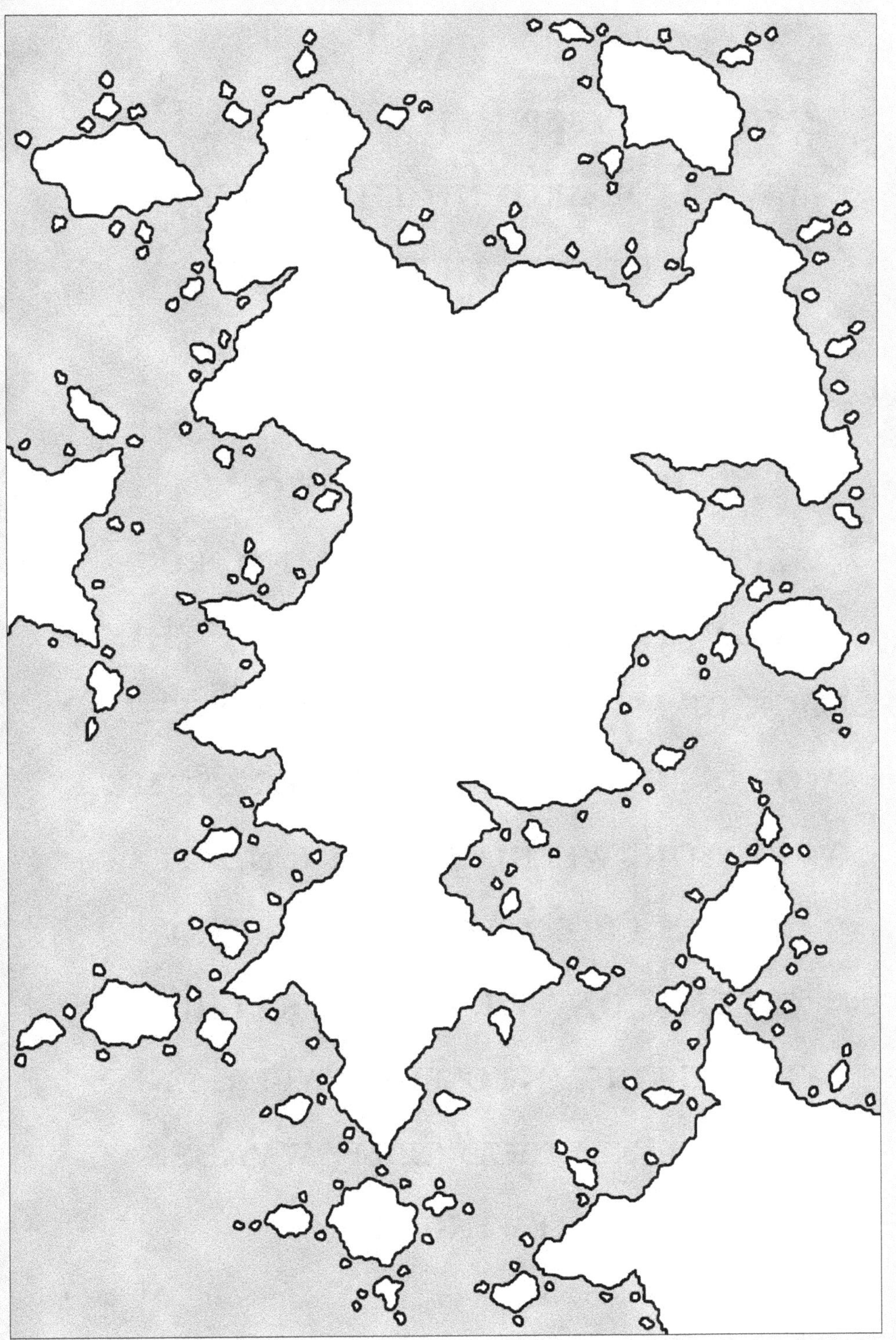

ANOTHER STEP I LIKE TO DO IS I'LL DRAW A LINE AROUND THE OUTSIDE OF THE ISLANDS IN THE WATER, SOMETIMES TWO OR THREE, DEPENDING ON WHAT I FEEL LIKE. THIS IS ANOTHER TECHNIQUE TO SEPARATE WATER FROM LAND, BUT AGAIN, I DO IT BECAUSE I LIKE THE LOOK OF IT. EXPERIMENT WITH WHAT WORKS BEST FOR YOU, BUT FOR SOME REASON, WITHOUT THE LINE, IT LOOKS LIKE THE ISLAND IS JUST SITTING ON THE WATER, RATHER THAN GOING INTO THE WATER, AND THE LINES CHANGE MY WAY OF VIEWING IT.

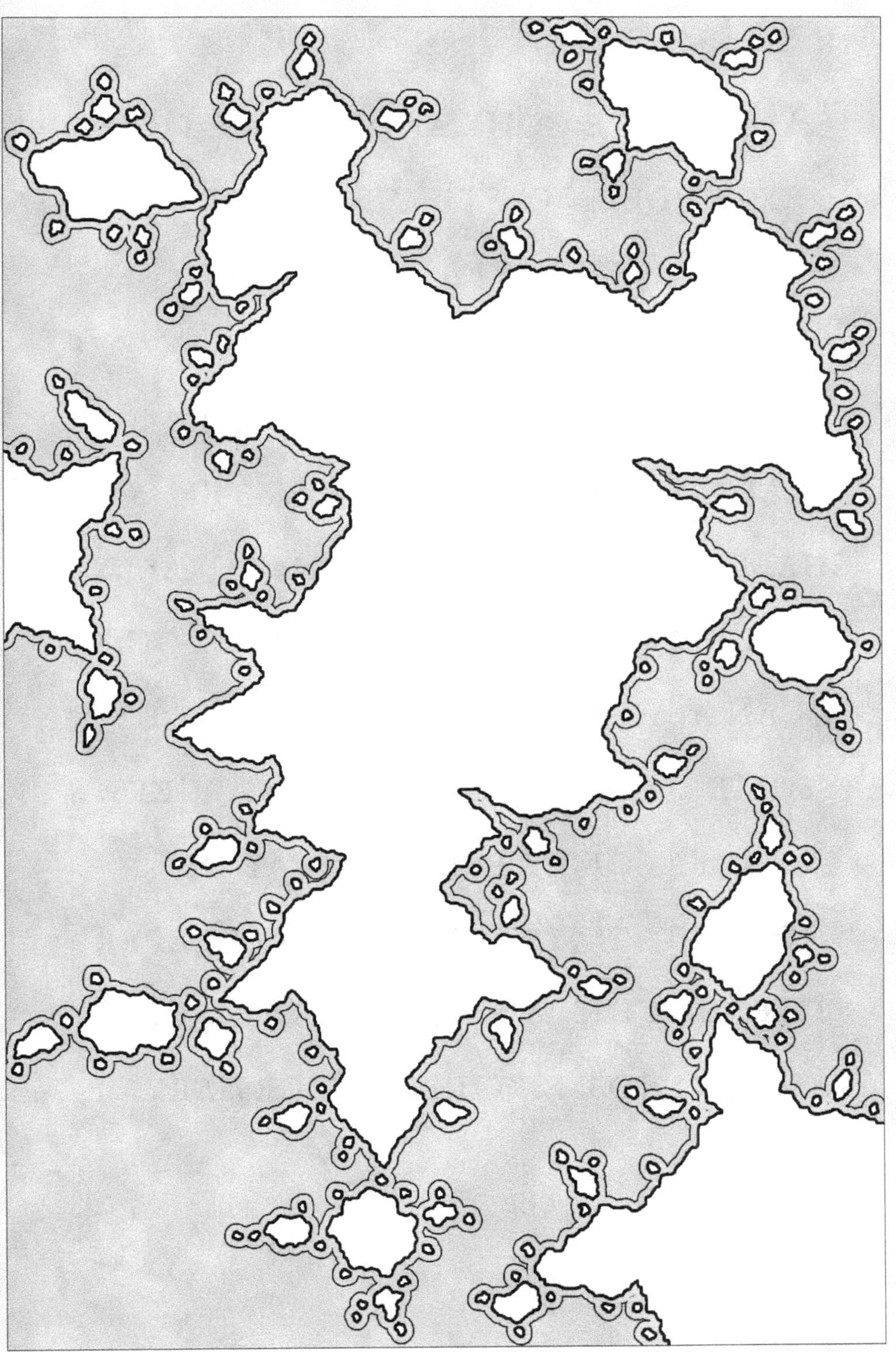

After I've gone and drawn the extended coast line, I like to shade the area to be a gray lighter than my ocean but not all the way white. To me, this represents where the water is shallow (since water is naturally shallower near the land). You can also take the time to add some darker patches to larger areas of water, as a way of showing that the water is deeper there. This is a cool touch, but again, not entirely necessary.

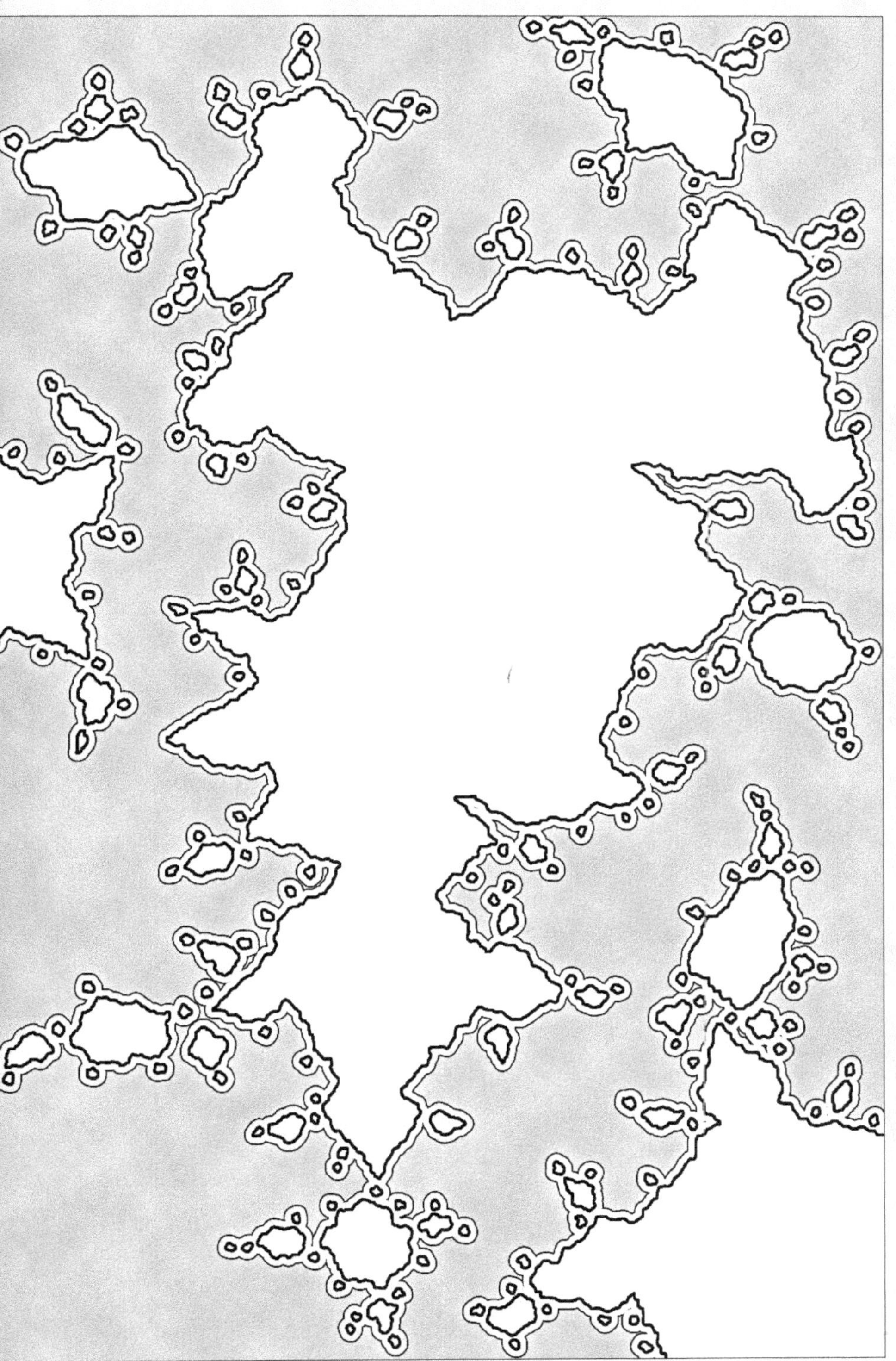

Mountains

Mountains are a really cool feature to maps, but also one of the more challenging aspects, in my opinion. In general, drawing mountains on a map is to note where they are, and that they exist, but not necessarily the size of specific mountains.

In the next few pages, I'm going to show you three styles of mountains, all of which I like, increasing in complexity.

Option 1: Basic Pyramid

Step 1: Draw a triangle with an open base.

Step 2: Add more, connecting them as shown.

Step 3: Add a ridge line to each mountain.

Step 4: Color in one side, leaving the base a little messy.

These mountains are good if you do want to draw and identify specific mountains, since they're easy to vary in size.

Option 2: Continuous Ridgeline

Step 1: Draw a diagonal squiggly line.

Step 2: Where the squiggle juts to the left, draw a ridge line to the left. Where it goes to the right, draw it to the right.

Step 3: Add smaller ridge lines for texture.

Step 4: Shade one side.

This is great for making a lot of mountains quickly, or for covering an area easily.

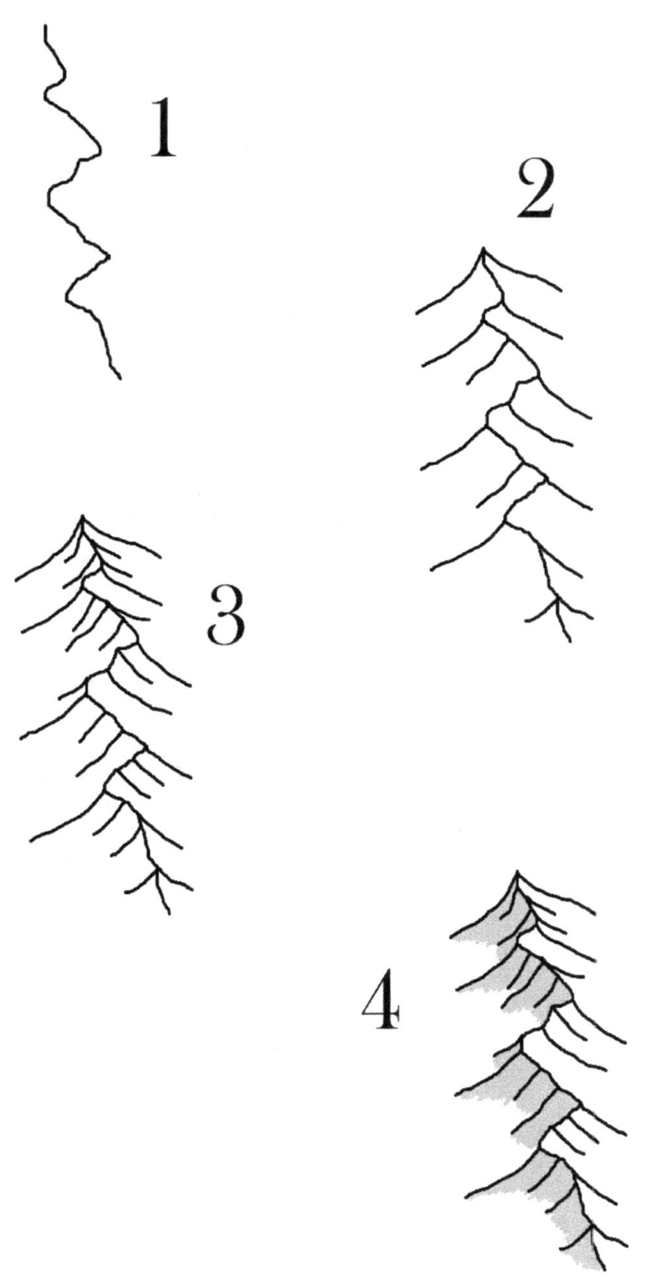

1
2
3
4

Option 3: Pyramid Ridgeline

Step 1: Draw a jagged pyramid

Step 2: Draw more, like you did in Basic Pyramid Step 2.

Step 3: Add smaller pyramids and draw ridgelines connecting pyramids.

Step 4: Add ridgelines like with the Continuous Ridgeline Step 2 and 3 and Basic Pyramid Step 3

Step 5: Shade in one side

This is the most artistic to me, and also the way to make the fullest mountain ranges.

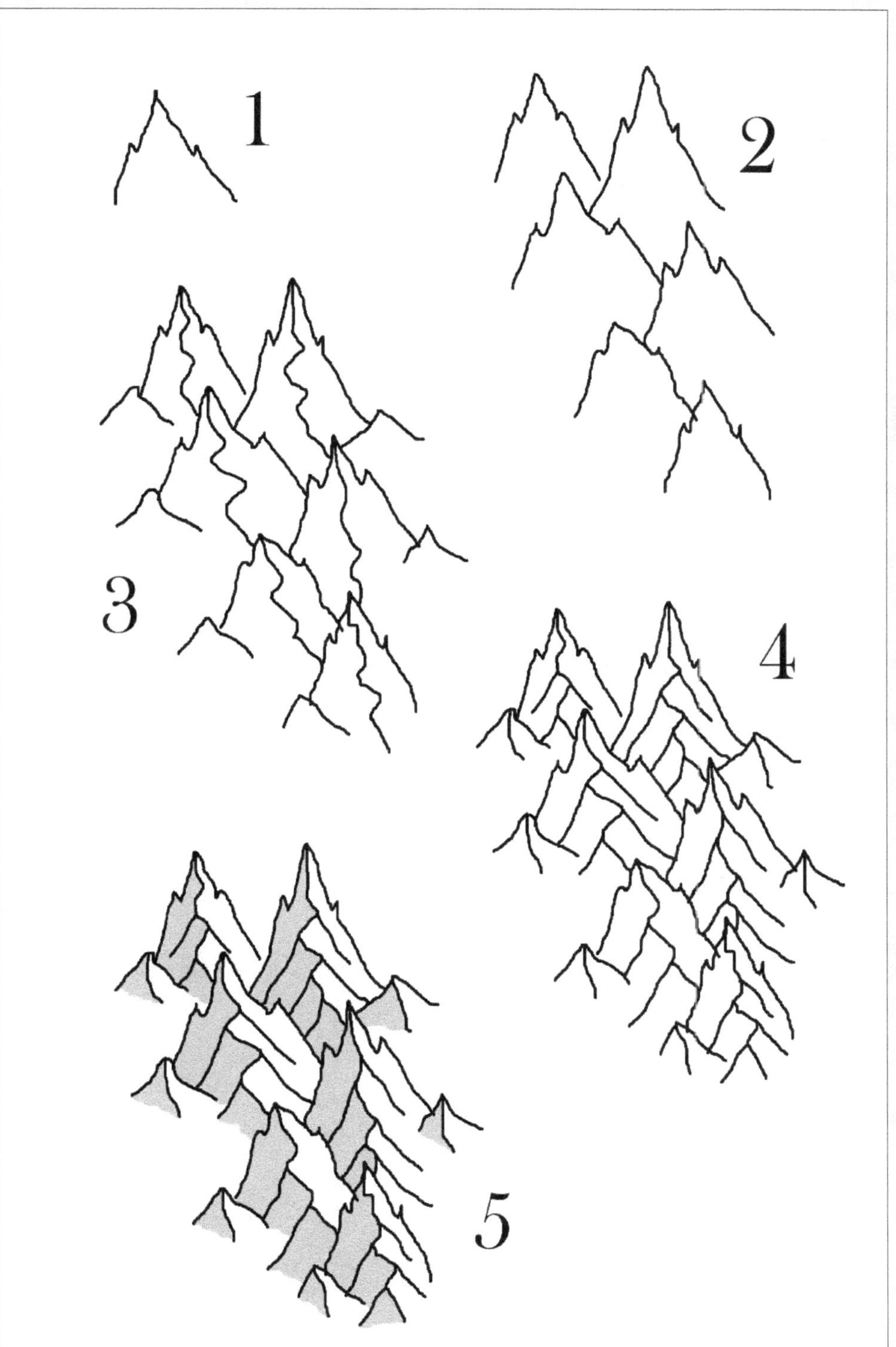

1
2
3
4
5

For the sake of the map I'm using for demonstration, I'm going with Option 3. Experiment with what you like, what works best for your style, and what works best with the look you're trying to convey.

I'm also not putting mountains everywhere. Later on, I may decide that I want more mountains, but for now, I'm content keeping them in the northern area.

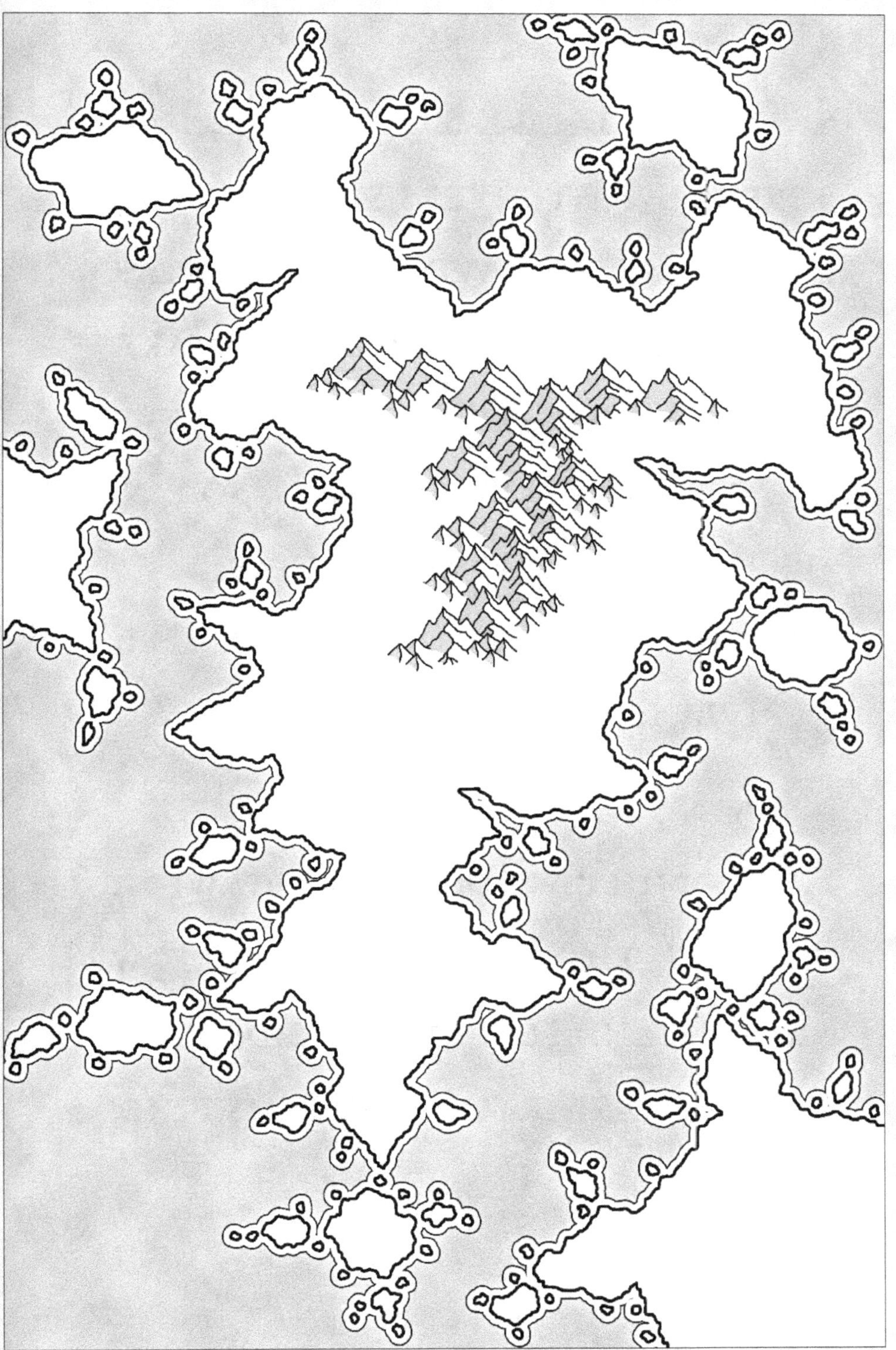

Now that I have mountains, I add rivers. Most rivers start in the mountains, so having a river start at a mountain on your map makes logical sense. Rivers run down to the ocean and end in bays, so find a bay and end it there. Tributaries are often smaller rivers, so they can be drawn smaller.

Also, while we don't know what the elevation is in the middle, we know land slopes towards the ocean, so starting there is fine.

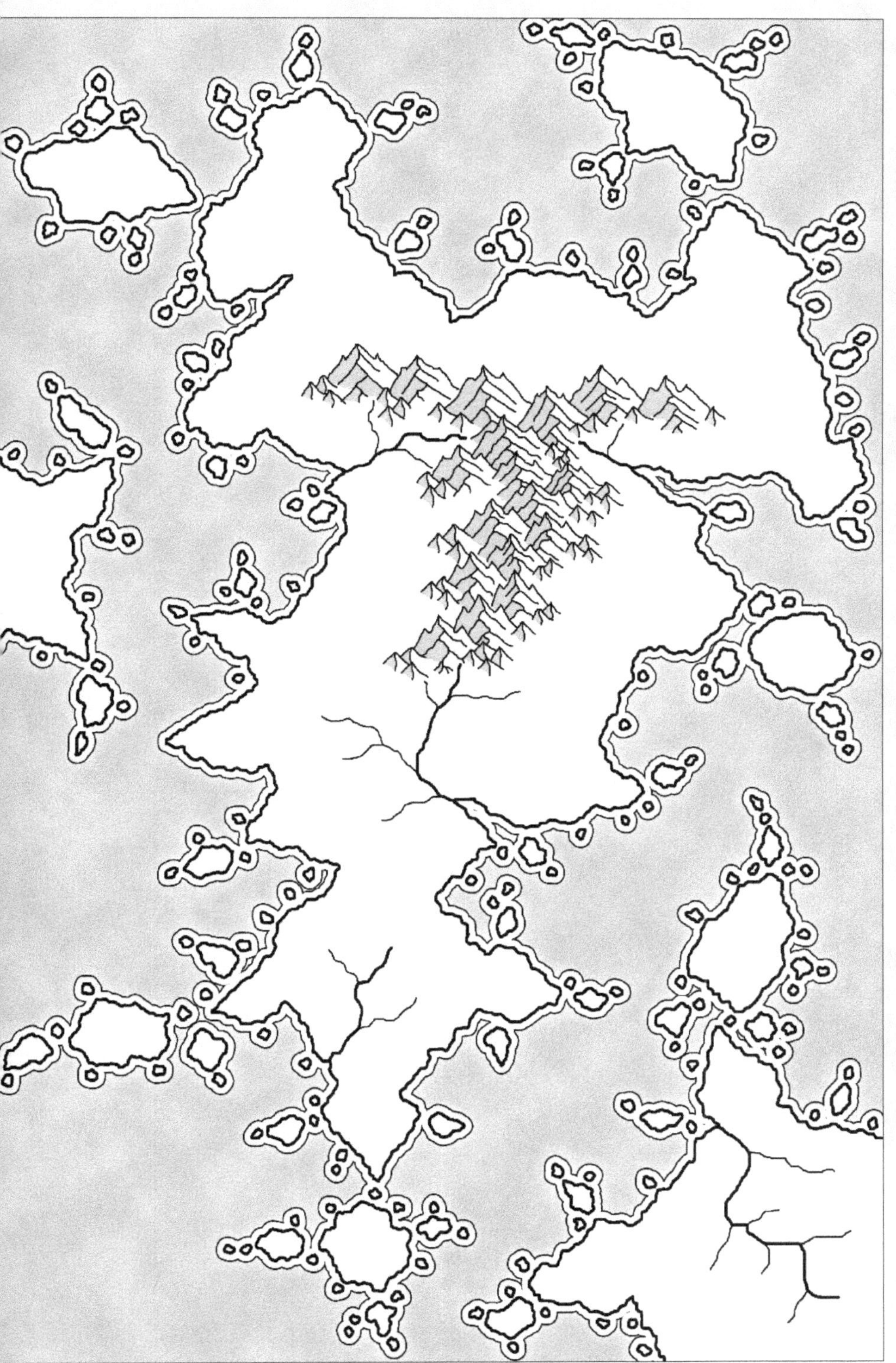

Trees and Forests

Trees and forests, while important to landscapes, can often be depicted by just coloring an area differently, like a darker green with lighter green being grasslands. Therefore, they're less necessary than other elements, but I think they add to the map, so I include them.

There are many ways to do forests, but I tend to do only two different types: deciduous and coniferous.

I keep it simple by having one tree
be bushy and another be taller
and skinnier. Then I place the
trees on a map in a hexagonal grid
style, where one tree overlaps
two trees. I can pack more of the
narrow trees together, giving
the impression of a dense spruce
or pine forest, and I make the
"leafy" trees lighter than the
"needle" trees because
coniferous trees tend to be
darker in color.

One thing I want to point out, over the next three pictures, all of the trees are the same, but they're all different sizes. With smaller trees, the forests are denser, but you also have to make more of them. There is a fine line between too big and too small, and a lot of what is right comes down to how big the map is. With maps that feature a really small area, bigger trees work well. If the area is the size of a continent, too big looks off.

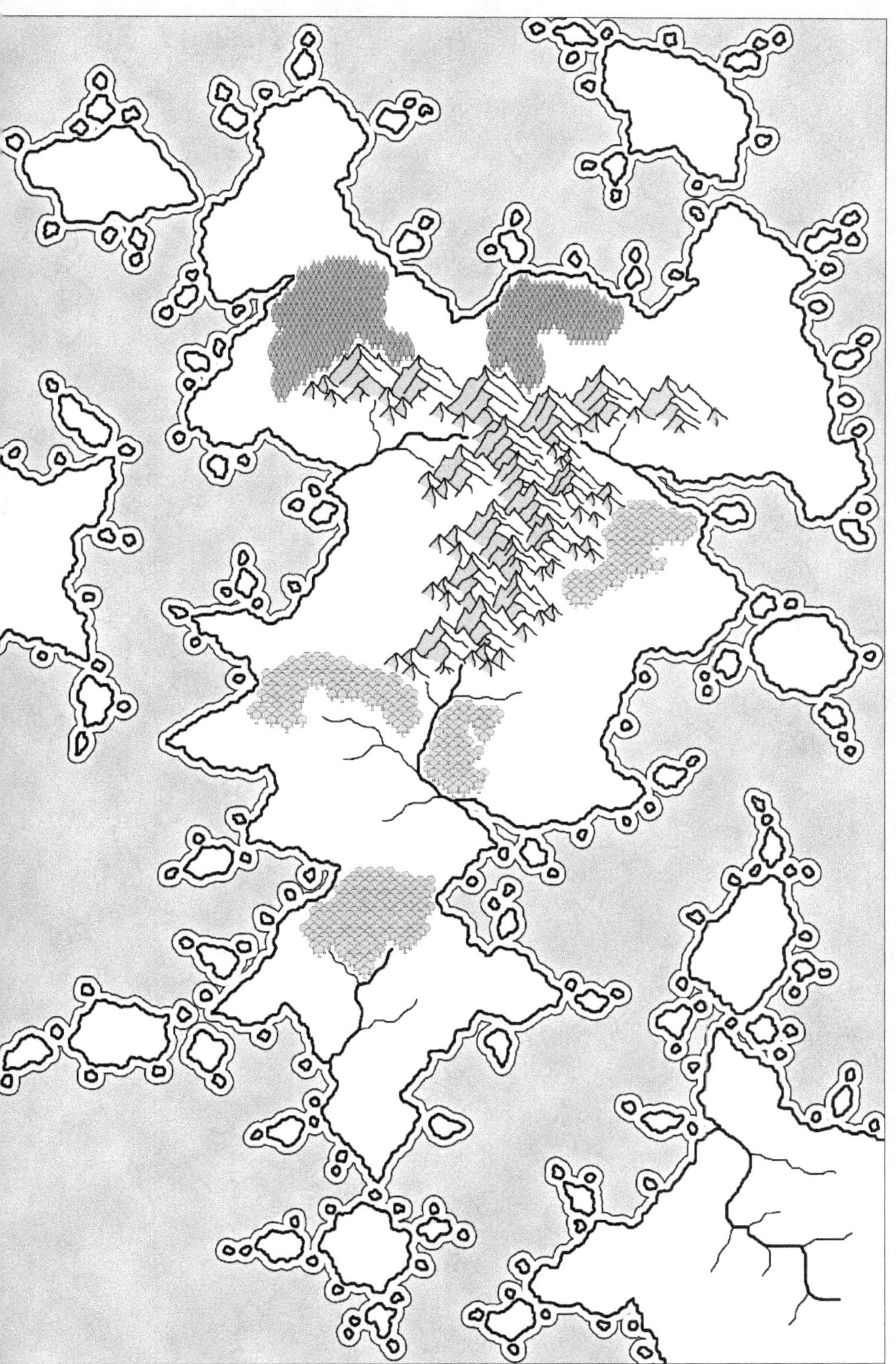

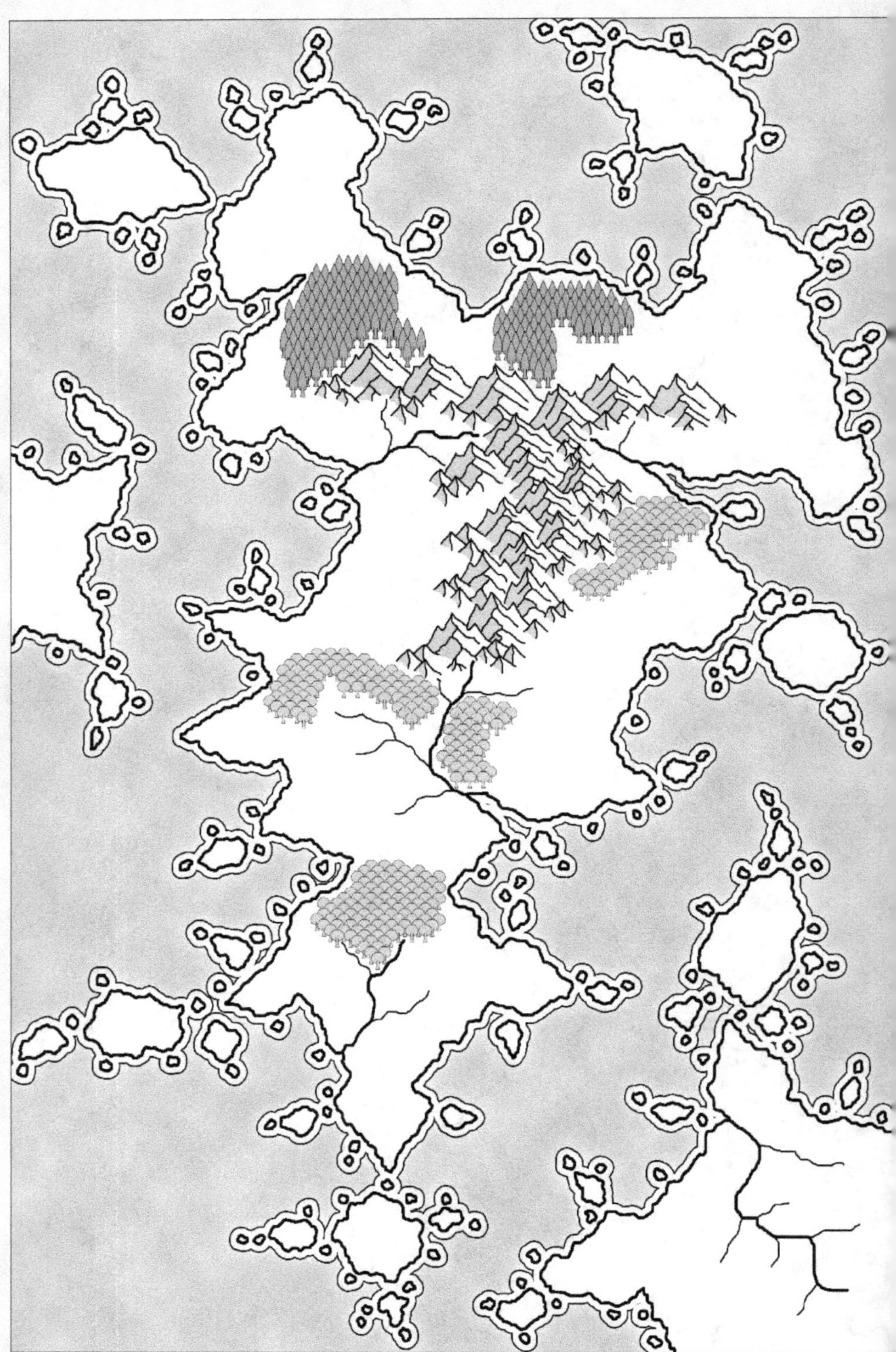

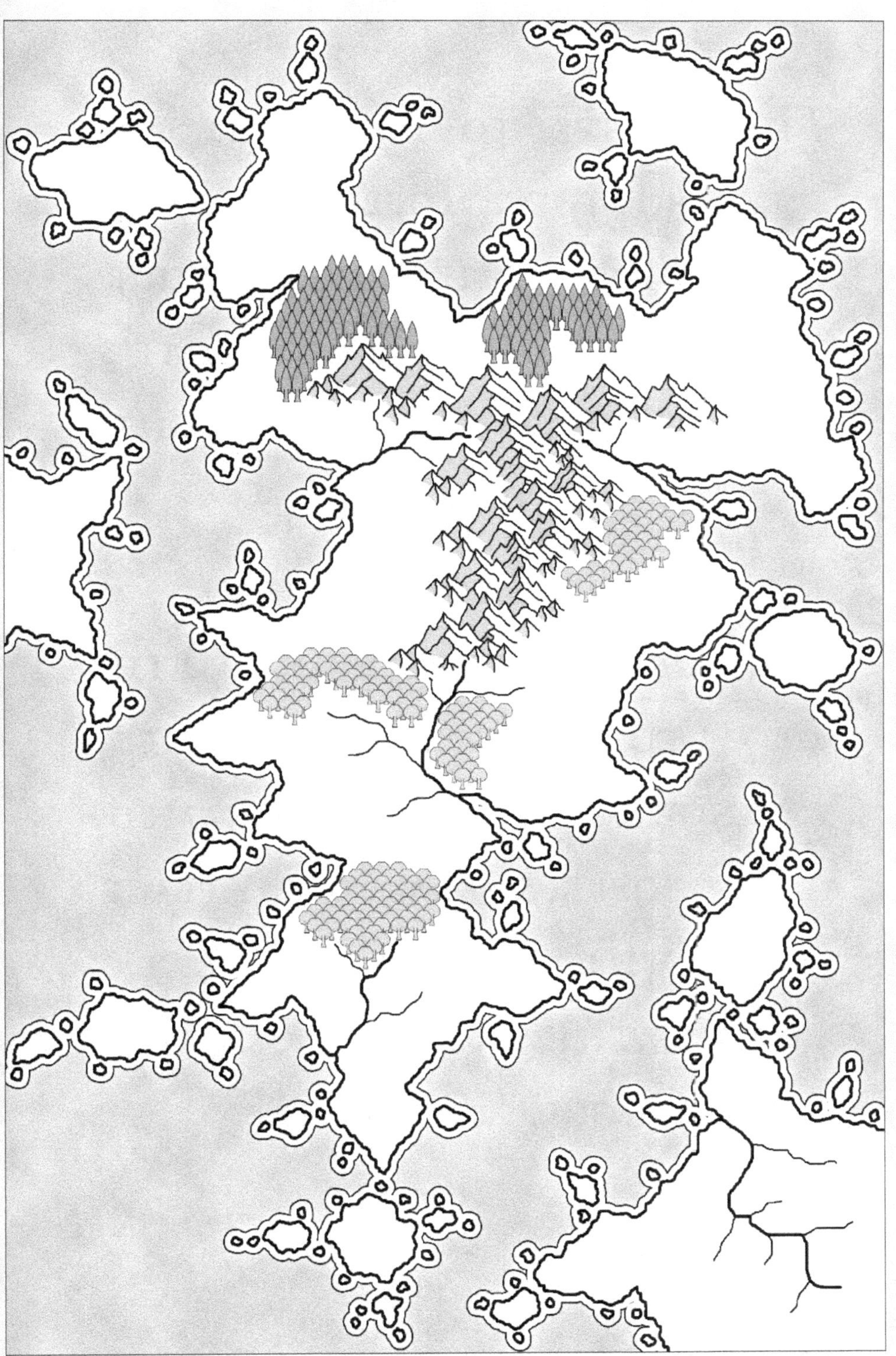

The last step to making a map is naming stuff. Hopefully you already have some names of your places in mind, but if not, that's alright; I have a tip that might help.

I like my names to mean something and be relevant to the map or to the story. In real life, we know places are often named after people, so some of my place names will be named like that. Other times... I just turn to Google Translate.

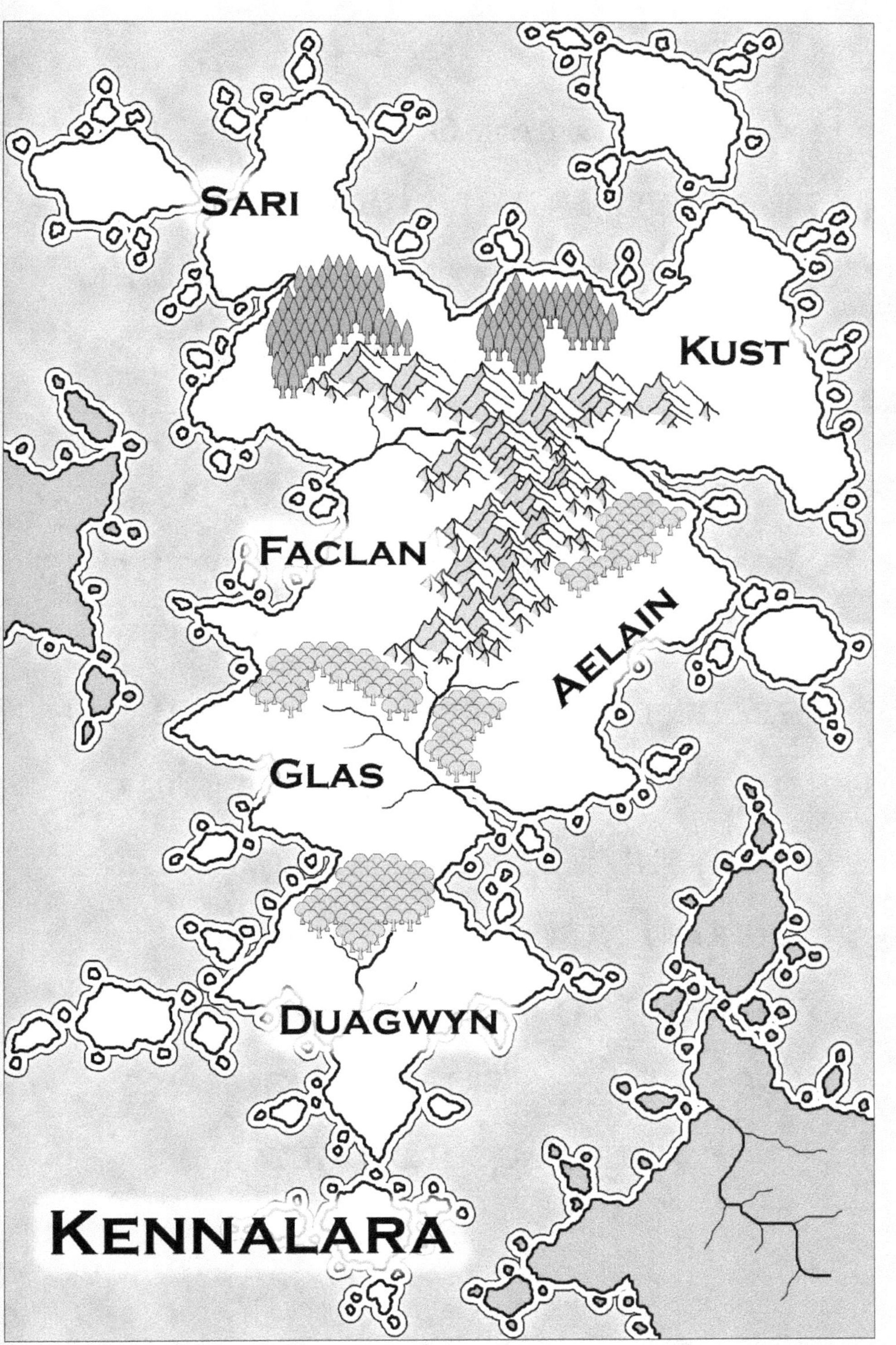
SARI
KUST
FACLAN
AELAIN
GLAS
DUAGWYN
KENNALARA

In Google Translate (just type in translate in the Google search bar), I look up various words, like courage, fire, peace, hope, etc. and then see what it translates into in different languages. Sometimes I don't like how the word looks, so I just move on to the next. Other times I combine multiple words to make it look good, and I did this for our map here. I also do this when I'm wanting to name characters. I look up an attribute and name them accordingly.

<u>Kennalara</u> I created by combining a couple words, specifically kenna and laera in Icelandic, which means "teach" and "learn" respectively. I figured a map about learning how to create maps would fit a name like that.

<u>Duagwyn</u> I created from the Welsh words meaning "black and white."

<u>Glas</u> I got when I typed in "gray" and had it translated into Scottish-Gaelic.

AELAIN I got from the Scottish-Gaelic word for "art," but while it's technically supposed to be Ealain instead of Aelain, I flipped the "a" and "e" to fit my aesthetic.

FACLAN I got from Scottish-Gaelic, and it means "words."

KUST is a translation for "coast" in Swedish.

SARI I got from the Finnish word for "island," which is "saari," and then dropped the middle "a."

You'll also notice that some of the land is gray while the rest is white. This is because those areas aren't part of the nation, but the reader can see they exist and are part of another part of the world.

And really, that's about it. Going further, you can create cities and towns, you can label mountain ranges and rivers, you can turn the nations into larger groups of countries. The only limit is your imagination. Best of luck, and happy world building!

Reference Guides

Character Name______________________________

Race/Species________________________________

Age___________ Height___________ Weight___________

Hair Color____________ Eye Color____________

Skin Color______________ Dominant Hand______

Nationality__________________________________

Tattoos/Scars_______________________________

Notable Physical Features____________________

____

Birthplace__________________________________

Parents_____________________________________

Siblings____________________________________

Current Residence___________________________

Occupation__________________________________

Notable Skills______________________________

____

Virtues_____________________________________

Flaws_______________________________________

Friends_____________________________________

Rivals/Enemies______________________________

Main Goal___________________________________

Character Name____

Race/Species____

Age____________ Height____________ Weight__________

Hair Color______________ Eye Color________________

Skin Color______________ Dominant Hand________

Nationality____

Tattoos/Scars____

Notable Physical Features______________________________

____

Birthplace____

Parents____

Siblings____

Current Residence______________________________________

Occupation____

Notable Skills____

____

Virtues____

Flaws____

Friends____

Rivals/Enemies____

Main Goal____

Name of Country

____

Ruler/Leader

____

Symbol or Flag

Type of Government _________________________

Notable Lords and Ladies or people of authority

____

____

____

National Colors _________________________

Notable Landmarks _________________________

____

____

Capital City _________________________

Major Cities _________________________

____

____

____

Guilds (if any) _________________________

____

____

Notable other Characters _________________________

____

____

____

NAME OF COUNTRY

____

RULER/LEADER

____

SYMBOL OR FLAG

TYPE OF GOVERNMENT _______________________________

NOTABLE LORDS AND LADIES OR PEOPLE OF AUTHORITY

____

____

____

NATIONAL COLORS _______________________________

NOTABLE LANDMARKS _______________________________

____

____

CAPITAL CITY _______________________________

MAJOR CITIES _______________________________

____

____

____

GUILDS (IF ANY) _______________________________

____

____

NOTABLE OTHER CHARACTERS _______________________________

____

____

____

Name of City _______________________________

Ruler/Leader _______________________________

Type of Government _______________________________

Size of City _______________________________

Notable Buildings and Locations _______________________________

____

____

____

Key Groups _______________________________

____

____

Notable Characters _______________________________

____

____

____

____

____

Other details to Remember

____

____

____

____

____

____

____

Name of City _______________________________

Ruler/Leader _______________________________

Type of Government _______________________________

Size of City _______________________________

Notable Buildings and Locations _______________________________

____

____

____

Key Groups _______________________________

____

____

Notable Characters _______________________________

____

____

____

____

____

Other details to Remember

____

____

____

____

____

____

____